# Mine to Choose

## Sue Schaeffer

Illustrated by Wilma Shelton Bell

*Start at page 63*

**Radiant** BOOKS

Gospel Publishing House/Springfield, Mo. 65802

02-0553

© 1979 by the Gospel Publishing House
Springfield, Missouri   65802
All rights reserved
Library of Congress Catalog Card No. 78-73144
ISBN 0-88243-553-1
Printed in the United States of America

A Leader's Guide for individual or group study with this book is
available from the Gospel Publishing House. Order number 32-
0227.

# Contents

# Chapter One

"There is a world in every head," my friend's mother used to say. I believe her.

You have dreams of the future, exciting plans, things you want to do, places you want to go and see, ideas of what you want to be—options, alternatives, preferences, issues, questions, selections, and choices—all your life.

But you really don't mind having it your way, do you? If you could just know you were equipped for it.

I started a conversation one day with a lovely teenage girl whom I didn't know. (As I'm apt to do almost anywhere, anytime.) Instead of the subject I wanted to pursue with her being awkward or boring, as I had suspected, it turned out to be a "delight insight," a happy happening! She came alive as we talked.

"Do you like to make your own decisions, or do you prefer a little help?" I asked her.

"You mean about what I wear, choosing my friends, or whom I date and that sort of thing?" she said.

"Yes," I nodded, "that's what I mean."

"Well," she replied with a mysterious little grin, "I don't mind guidance from my parents and maybe advice from my counselor at school on some things, but usually I want to decide myself. I like to make up my own mind."

IT'S YOUR WORLD!

*So this is the thinking of a young mind*—I reflected. *Tell me more.*

"Do girls still talk about marrying and having a family," I ventured, "or do most favor a good-paying job or a career?"

"Oh, no!" she stated emphatically. "All the girls I know want to meet the 'right guy' when the time comes, marry, and have a family."

As she excused herself to leave and darted from the room, I sensed life's *greatest* choices were tumbling around in her small head. For her, and for you, most of the big decisions are yet to be made.

## MULTIPLE CHOICE GAME

In a book I read recently, *Dr. Rubin, Please Make Me Happy* (T. I. Rubin [New York: Arbor House

Publishing Co., 1974]), the author compares the mind to a tape recorder or electronic computer that distills, records, and transmits enormous quantities of information and feelings. "A most magnificent and complicated structure," he calls it; making choices and decisions which, in turn, lead to actions and countless varieties of human experiences.

Let's talk about this. These messages leading to choices, and those choices leading to actions can become quite a puzzling game.

When did the game of "multiple choice" first begin? For you, it was probably choosing a toy or selecting a book when you were very small.

"Hurry, make up your mind, dear! Which one?"

Remember? But the game started long before that.

## *I wonder if God's back is turned?*

There was a woman named Eve who lived in the very beginning of the existence of this world. God created Eve and her husband Adam as perfect people. He also gave them a faculty or ability called free will.

You've heard the story from the first Book of the Bible, how temptations and questions came to Eve. She had to decide whether to obey God and maintain her relationship with Him or disregard His instructions and satisfy her own desires.

She chose to eat the forbidden fruit. Then she wasn't happy until she persuaded someone else to sin. This seems to be the norm, doesn't it? She had someone to share the blame, then—her husband. As they stood before God—the two of them—they both tried to shift the blame.

"The woman *You gave me* told me to . . . ," Adam blamed God.

blamed the devil, "The serpent beguiled (deceived) me. . . ."

God didn't accept these excuses. He fixed the blame directly where it belonged—on the individual.

Eve rationalized or explained her behavior on the grounds of, "If it is good to eat, what's wrong with eating it?" She was drawn away of her own craving and didn't ask for help in her temptation. Sin came because Eve desired to do something forbidden. Satan used what was available. He hasn't changed.

You aren't born with Eve's or Adam's sin. But you are born with a sinful nature because they started sin. And when you bump headfirst into the adult world you're going to discover the influences of sin.

Sin is simply transgressing or breaking God's laws. Have you ever noticed what is in the middle of *sin*? It's always *I*. When you break God's law, the burden of guilt sets in—sometimes immediately, sometimes later. The human symptoms of guilt appear as remorse, regret, and anguish.

It is sometimes fashionable and acceptable to deny the reality of right and wrong in an attempt to quiet guilt. But only at the price of destroying all values. You wouldn't want that, would you?

I know parents who tried denying the reality of right and wrong in the sad case of their unmarried daughter. After three abortions, to save the family name, the wretched, wrecked life of their teenager exposed a mask worn thin and ragged; showing the deep human struggle that guilt renders.

The girl blamed the parents, "If they would only let me marry him!"

The parents blamed the boy, "If he would leave town there would be no problem!"

I SEE ME!

9

The boy blamed circumstances, "If I made enough money we could get married."

Blame circled around and . . . boomerang! The arrow of guilt shot back to the already laden girl. How I wish I could have reached her sooner before the weight bent her low. I would have told her how Jesus forgives our failures and sins and erases the deep-rooted bitterness caused by misunderstandings and unpleasant experiences, and He eases the hurt.

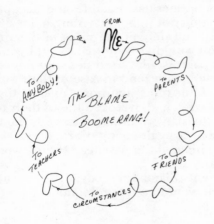

Although "literature, the mirror to life" says no remedy for guilt is known to man, Shakespeare erred. The Scriptures declare to guilty persons that Jesus lived their life (except for sinning) and died their death that by way of exchange they might be credited with His life and righteousness. By a simple act of grace our believing in the resurrected Lord Jesus brings us into a new life.

*Christ was made what He was not . . . That we might be made what we are not!*

According to William Tyndale, these truths constitute the "good, glad, and merry tidings, which make a man's heart sing, and his feet to dance for joy." What a trade for an ugly, heavy guilt pack!

# R<sub>x</sub> FOR CURE!

A vital question for everyone is: "How can I be reconciled to God, after I've failed and broken His rules?" Or, put another way: "Is there a cure for the awful guilt I feel and the desire to keep doing things that bring guilt?"

Our acceptance of Christ brings freedom from sin's guilt and from sin's power. This is called *salvation*. It means you are not only forgiven for any and all past un-Christlike actions, but you also receive power not to commit these same sins again. Isn't that marvelous?

Salvation is

DELIVERANCE

from SIN

and PENALTY!

The word *salvation* implies the ideas of deliverance, safety, preservation, healing, and soundness. Salvation is the great inclusive word of the gospel and Christ extends it to all as a gift of grace!

One Bible scholar points out that:

1. The believer *has been* saved from the guilt and penalty of sin and is safe.

2. The believer *is being* saved from the habit and dominion of sin.

3. The believer *is to be saved* in the sense of entire conformity to Christ.

Life is a journey. Roads head every direction. At a crossroads, a point we all come to at one time or another, the paths may not be plainly marked. An "almost straight" road, you see, is a deceptive lure. Sign posts, hidden down the way, tell of the danger.

THIS WAY IS ALMOST STRAIGHT....

WON'T IT GET ME THERE?

Two incidents, both happening at crossroads, which I don't feel is coincidental, illustrate the chief choice of life.

The first event happened to me during a visit in another state. I smiled at two young girls as I entered a crowded bookstore. Passing the occult section where the girls were seriously scanning a large book, I started on to the religious book rack. Glancing over my shoulder I noticed the girls still looking at me.

We eye-wrestled for a split second and on impulse I stepped toward them.

"Hi!" I said, opening the conversation (as I told you earlier I'm likely to do anytime, anywhere).

"I'm doing research on the occult for my high school class," I told them a little nervously. "I have a briefcase of material, books, tapes, articles, and records. Do you understand much about it?"

This turned them on. We began to chat. It was strange. I felt icy vibes but the chatting was warm and flowing.

One of the girls was quite attractive. She did most of the talking. All of a sudden she snapped at me, "I don't believe in God!" Her long black hair swished forward, framing her gorgeous, delicate face.

I had not, at that point, mentioned God.

"You just told me," I inserted, "that you have these supernatural powers and you always know when something bad is going to happen."

"Yeah," she spurted, "I do. I see different colored lights flashing and there are other ways I can tell, too! I inherited these powers from my grandmother." The atmosphere was getting heavy.

"All supernatural powers," I contradicted, "come either from God or Satan. Are you aware of that?"

I found myself in a corner, but instantly I sent up an unspoken prayer. She turned to me almost angrily and said, "God sent you here, didn't He?"

And after she had just told me she didn't believe in God! Here was my chance. I didn't answer her question. I think we both knew.

A few minutes of gentle persuasion, directed by the Holy Spirit, convinced her to give Jesus a chance at her mixed-up life. Amazingly, she handed the book on witchcraft to her friend and went with me, hand-in-hand, outside to a bench where we prayed.

"Oh! I feel so clean!" she kept saying, squeezing my hand harder and harder. ". . . and at peace for once in my life." Her tears were real.

About that time our group came looking for me and we left. I was nearly speechless, but as we neared the car I asked, "What is the name of this new mall?"

"The Crossroads," someone answered casually.

My other experience was across the ocean at the "Crossroads of the World," Panama. In the plaza, with its palm-lined, flower-decked walkways, a young Panamanian strolled directly toward me. He was in sad condition—a member of the drug scene. I thrust a tract into his hand but with distrust and disgust he threw it on the ground, spat at it, turned his back, and walked away. The haunting pang of this memory will never leave me.

In both cases, a teenager made a critical choice. Now you are at a crossroads. What's your choice? It is your world!

Dear God, the greatest choice ever made was when You sent Your Son to save me. In my world of decisions I have decided to invite Him into my heart and life. Together we can make all the other choices. *Amen.*

... **PLEASE!** ...

**YOUR OPINION** ... ... **WE? ?**

What do these scriptures
mean to you?

1. JOHN 1:8
2. ISAIAH 1:18
3. I. JOHN 1:9
4. EPHESIANS 2:8

**3** QUESTIONS -- **3** MINUTES!

❀ you can say a lot in 60 seconds! ❀

**1.**
In your opinion, what is
a Christian?

**2.**
Why be a Christian, anyway?

**3.**
How do you get to be a Christian?

# Chapter Two

*Little Miss Muffet*
*Sat on a tuffet,*
*Eating her curds and whey;*
*There came a big spider,*
*Who sat down beside her,*
*And frightened Miss Muffet away.*

"Nursery rhymes are important educational tools," says a child psychologist, quoted in a local newspaper. It would be an education of sorts to learn what a tuffet or curds and whey are—wouldn't it?

Little Miss Muffet's real name was *Patience*, I learned from my newspaper. Her father, Dr. Thomas Muffet, studied and wrote about spiders in the late 1500's.

"Spiders? Eeeek!" is probably your reaction!

Spiders are not a favorite topic, I know. Especially with girls. To be honest with you, I'm afraid of them too. Certain times of the year they get in my bathtub and in corners here and there. But the writer who enlightened me about Little Miss Muffet also informs us that a spider might be appealing. (See *A Spider Might* by Tom Walther [New York: Charles Scribner's Sons, 1978].)

I can't bring myself to see it that way, although their antics do prove to be quite a performance. If a spider is found stuck in the bathtub, Walther

suggests he be given a lift to a safer place with a piece of paper. But I find it less frightening to run water down the drain as quickly as possible!

Don't you get a bit spooked when your face becomes entangled in a cobweb or a spider dangles from the ceiling and lands in your hair? I think most of us associate spiders with fear, even though researchers tell us they are not nature's villains at all.

As we take a look at finding your place in the church, I think we can see a parallel between the spider and responsibility. There seems to be a speck of fear in most girls when they are first approached to fill a responsible position or become active in the church. What causes this fear? Is it reasonable or justifiable?

A Mother Goose rhyme for teens might go something like this:

*Little Miss Lou Lou*
*Sat on a church pew,*
*Biting her nails with dread;*
*Along came her pastor,*
*And he simply asked her*
*To help share the load, so she fled!*

Before we can explore this complex network of delicate threads spun by our "spider" of responsibility or involvement, a few issues concerning the church must be clarified. Some of these areas are found in the following questions.

1. What is the church? 2. How does my church help me? 3. What do I contribute to my church? 4. What do I expect from my church? 5. Is there a place in the church for me? 6. Do I have some basic hangups? 7. Why go to church?

The Church is not just a building. Nor is it an ordinary group of people. It is a very special Body made up of very special people. It is the body of Christ and He is the Head. If you accepted the salvation we talked about in the first chapter, you are a part of that special body of Christ, the Church, and you are very special!

A congregation of worshipers or a particular denomination of Christians is also called a church. Let's look at the local assembly of Christians, gathered to worship, serve, and win others, and *your* place in that church.

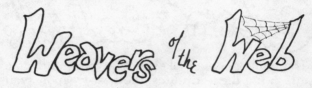

An estimated 80 million Americans choose not to participate in or be affiliated with organized churches. Dr. J. Russell Hale of Lutheran Theological Seminary at Gettysburg, Pennsylvania traveled from coast to coast, interviewing people of various educational, social, and economic backgrounds—all of them outside the church.

He classifies them into several types:

1. The "anti-institutionalists," people who reject organizational structures as useless to "true religion."

2. The "boxed-in," people who have quit the church because it was too confining.

3. The "burned-out," people who feel wearied and drained by church work.

4. The "cop-outs," people who are never really involved in church life.

5. The "happy hedonists," people who find fulfillment in pleasures. "It's either church or recreation, and recreation wins," some commented.

6. The "locked-out," including those who have felt rejected, neglected, or discriminated against by churches.

Now you know the major qualms of the un-churched of America. I wanted you to see the different snares that are lurking out there for you.

"I'll never abandon the church," you're saying.

But at times you may be tempted to join ranks with the "anti-institutionalists," the "boxed-in," the "burned-out," the "cop-outs," the "happy hedonists," or the "locked-out."

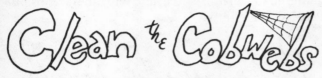

If the thought ever takes root in your mind, go to battle using the Scriptures, the best weapon available. Throughout the years I've claimed several verses in the Bible as my favorites. Three Scripture passages I go back to over and over again are the following:

> Now unto him that is able to do exceeding abundantly above all that we ask or think, according to the power that worketh in us (Ephesians 3:20).

The secret to me in that verse is, "according to the power that worketh in us"—the Holy Spirit.

> These things have I spoken unto you, that my joy might remain in you, and that your joy might be full (John 15:11).

The context of this verse unlocks the message for me: abiding in Christ and Christ abiding in me. A whole chapter could be written about the vine, the branches, and the fruit of John 15.

> Looking unto Jesus the author and finisher of our faith . . . (Hebrews 12:2).

As I look to Jesus I like to think He authors my faith—chapter by chapter of my life—from beginning to end and all the pages in between!

MY
FAVORITE
SCRIPTURES:

_____
_____
_____
_____
_____
_____
_____
_____
_____
_____
_____
_____
_____

Your church helps you grow and be healthy by teaching you the Word, more than by any other way. You can count on the Scriptures to be your most dependable guide in conflict. Here's how: As you read the Bible and allow it to "soak" in or saturate you, it's like the gentle hand of someone who really cares for you placing a Band-Aid on your heart. Or, that special someone whispering in your ear, telling you everything is going to be all right. Your hurts and discomforts give way to a calm composure that is unlike you. You are at peace with yourself.

There are actually three relationships going on in your life at all times. Your relationship to God, your relationship to others, and your relationship to yourself. When these relationships are in order, you will want to contribute what you can to your church.

First, your prayer life will change. You will *want* to pray more. Before you know it, you'll be knocking the old cobwebs out of the way and having the time of your life! But you'll have to watch out for spiderlings (baby spiders), to keep the cobwebs cleared away. You can do this as you grow.

When you tell a friend, "I had the best time at church today!" and she asks, "How come?" you can answer: "I took care of the nursery, our attendant was ill." Or, "I told a story in children's church and a little kid about 10 years old came forward for prayer." Or, "I sang in the choir and a little old grandmother told me it thrilled her to see me there."

Your friend may never know, but you will know: Your church helped you grow spiritually. And if you aren't asked to do anything specific, but you are faithful in attendance, willing, and active in the worship and activities, you are making great strides in your Christian growth.

I was shopping in a gift store one day, when the young salesgirl who was helping me told me how she found her place, as a brand-new Christian, in the church. She said her sisters in the Lord were busy, busy, singing in the choir, teaching classes, and playing the piano. This bothered her a great deal.

"I couldn't do any of that," she said. "But you know," she sighed, "I went to God in prayer about it and He revealed to me that I must be myself—unique, plain, dumb, and ugly as I am—He wants me to be me! He taught me that my smile and a 'listening ear' to people is a blessing to them. I feel it's my place in the church."

I'm glad God doesn't turn us out like gingerbread men on a cookie sheet. He made us different; so naturally we are going to act different. I like the assortment God has made.

Hang-Ups
(PART OF THE WEB)

What do you expect from your church? I *expect* that everyone expects something a little different.

But this I know, your expectations can be met by trying and can be swallowed up in happy, fulfilling Christian ministry in your local church.

I can hear you now. "My church is okay, but it could stand plenty of improvement."

Can you hear me?

You may well be the one to make those improvements! The church is never "they," it is "we." I would like to gently suggest that you hang up your "hang-ups" and help make the Body a compassionate, vibrant, powerful church.

I read the story of a man who in the weekly prayer meeting was always confessing the same sins. One day when he was praying he used this figure of speech:

"O Lord, since we last gathered, the cobwebs have come between us and Thee. Clear away the cobwebs that we may again see Thy face."

Then a brother called out, "O God, kill the spider!"

I hope you have learned or have been reminded of ways to stifle the "fear spider." I was amused by a card sent to my married daughter when she had minor surgery. A longtime friend of hers had chosen a get-well card with a small girl and a tiny spider on the front. Inside, it said, "How's your tuffet?" We got a good laugh from that card.

You have a choice to make. You can either cringe or cower from your imaginary spiders, while sitting on your "tuffet" doing nothing, or be up and about the Master's business, moving so fast that no spider could ever weave a web for you.

To Find My Place In The Church

# I WILL SERVE!

I WILL PRAY:

Dear God, there are many forces forever spinning cobwebs to hinder my doing much for you.... with your help, I'll keep them swept clean from now on, and as I find my place in the church, I will fill it faithfully.

...Amen.

I WILL READ:
Proverbs 29:25 R.S.V.

# Chapter Three

Hide 'n Seek

When you begin to think about the will of God—
*seeking* the will of God, *finding* the will of God, and
*being* in the will of God—what comes to your mind?

Do you think of a pious individual who seldom
smiles as one who would know God's will?

Do you think of the happy-go-lucky person as the
type who would know God's will?

Sometimes young people feel God's will is completely beyond them, or that it is "way out there"
somewhere in God's vast mystical universe, always
in the future.

How do you feel about God? Do you think He has
plans for your life? Does He care what happens to
you?

Of course, He cares. Just because you are one of
the younger children in His family doesn't mean you
are of no concern to Him. Your Heavenly Father
definitely loves you and watches over you—as much
as He does anyone, of any age, anywhere in the
world! He wants what is best for you. That's why you
should want to know how He can direct you, where
He wants to lead you, and when.

Christian young people are naturally expected to
seek God's will, but do you know how? Someone has
said finding God's will is sensing in spirit what's on
God's heart. Maybe you desire to know His perfect
will for your life "later"—in college, in marriage, for

the right job. You may not think it's important to know God's will *now*. It's all right to have your own way today. It's fun-and-game time.

One summer two of my nieces, ages 9 and 11, spent some time with me. About dusk each day they would insist on one last game of "Hide and Seek." One of the kids in the neighborhood would bury his head in his arms, lean on a tree, and start counting, "One-two-three . . . 57-58 . . . 90-91-92 . . . 99-100! Here I come with both eyes open!"

Every kid in his own private hiding place created the lull of deep silence until his chance when "Its" back was turned—then a dash to the tree, pat one-two-three, and safe!

Some of God's children play this game. God is "It." He hides His face while you scamper off and hide in your own private hiding place. Then when God's back is turned you run and check in, one-two-three. You never have anything to do with Him. You know He is around but that's about all. Then it's your turn to be "It." You wait about as long in prayer as it takes to count to 100 and then you go in search of God. Somewhere in the rush of the game He slips past you, one-two-three, and you fail to catch Him.

God's will is always within your reach when you seek properly for it. He doesn't want His children to be overanxious about tomorrow. There's no magic formula other than doing what you know you should

GOD SPEAKS:
INNER IMPRESSIONS
BIBLE
COMMON SENSE
COUNSELORS
CONSCIENCE

according to the light of the Word and listening for God's voice. He speaks by inner personal impressions, through someone who is unaware of your need, through a godly counselor, and often through your own common sense and your conscience. Your most reliable source is, of course, the Bible and your impressions from the Holy Spirit as you commune with the Lord.

THE SEARCH IS ON

How hard is it to find God's will? I would say it is about as hard to find God's will as you want to make it. It is a matter of attitude and of willingness to submit.

Ask yourself, "Do I sincerely want God's will or my own will for my life? Do I want God's will for all of my life or just part of my life? Do I want God's will all of the time or only part of the time? Am I ready to give up my will?"

When you set a pattern of following God's will it often turns out to be exactly what you like to do. He leads according to your talents and abilities, even when they are hidden from you. God wants you to be happy. He isn't going to direct you into anything you will be miserable doing. Remember that.

God's Will... REVEALED MESSIAH or CONCEALED

God has a perfect will and also what I call a circumstantial or permissive will. Much of His will is revealed in His Word. His messages there are for you. The principles, ideals, and concepts in the Bible are universal; they are for everyone. What isn't explained is revealed *after* you obey the commands in the Scriptures—believe on Jesus, confess your sins, be filled with the Holy Spirit, put on the whole armor of God, resist the devil, obey the Great Commission, and many other guidelines. God's will is a continuing experience that expands as you grow spiritually.

You can feel secure in God's perfect will even when you don't have the vaguest idea about your future. The secret (if there is a secret at all) is in walking, living, and doing what you know to be His will today. That, in turn, throws light on tomorrow.

"But what if I fail?" you ask. There's no rule that says when you fail you can never be in God's will again. It's well worth the effort to keep trying.

God's permissive will comes about either by your own lack of complete obedience or by some force out of your control which you have allowed to become too much a part of your life. That is why I call it His circumstantial will. Circumstances push you in a corner and you can't see God's will or you're forced to operate outside His will for a while. This could be caused by associates, such as friends, non-Christian relatives, or an undedicated companion, later in life. Or, this force could be habits or simply self-will.

My Christian walk has led me through some of the most exciting years. It started when I was 15. The Lord turned me around and since then the Holy Spirit has constantly been before me like a giant traffic light—red, green, and yellow. He shows me when to go, when to stop, and many times flashes the yellow caution light. His Word is "a light unto my path" (Psalm 119:105).

The first time I felt His guidance was the morning after I became a Christian and was filled with the Holy Spirit. I was getting ready for school. It was my sophomore year in high school. The Lord began to talk to my heart. I looked in the mirror and saw a new person. It was the first time my spirit bore witness with the Holy Spirit. I knew instantly what I must do, as a Christian, on several issues.

That day at school I had a voice in the student council meeting. I spoke against having a dance at a class party we were planning. I lost the vote but from that time on my classmates looked at me differently. They knew where I stood and the Lord showed me in a precious way that I could be a silent, "loud" witness—if you can figure that one out!

Since then it has never been very hard to get answers from the Lord. This sensitivity has grown because I do not fight against it. I have clearly felt the Holy Spirit's presence and guidance. This doesn't mean I never make mistakes. I've made many, but I always know what to do: I need to read my Bible and allow Christ to minister to me in my prayer life. I have never had to live with uncertainty for long.

His leading comes in steps—one at a time. I haven't always been aware of the preparatory training I was going through until suddenly another door would open and I would enter a new room filled with His wonders.

## Take One GIANT Step!

To illustrate this step-by-step strategy, the first thing I was asked to do as a teenage Christian was to lead the children in their singing. Then I became the substitute teacher for the junior boys, and I taught a class for a few years.

Then I began to feel a tugging I couldn't shake. I felt led to start a neighborhood Bible-story time, which I conducted faithfully until the Lord instructed me to extend it. The era of the bus ministry led me to parks and apartment complexes to present puppet shows proclaiming the gospel. One day a dirty-faced little boy climbed down out of a tree and knelt by my knee. As tears rolled down his cheeks, he said, "I don't know anything about Jesus." What a joy it was to be in God's will that day and lead a child to Him!

About that time I had a vision of a small white church in my left hand. I was praying at the time, and it was so real I could feel the weight of it in my hand. The Lord said to my heart, "You hold the church of tomorrow in your hand, the children." I didn't understand this fully until the next week when a minister invited me to come to his city and hold a Kid's Crusade. That started two summers of going into churches large and small. Then I was asked to teach children's church at a large convention.

The next step was a giant step. I was invited to go as a supervisor with a church youth group to Panama. My duties included everything *but* working with children. However, a strange thing occurred shortly after we arrived and I found myself in the perfect position to tell those darling black children about Jesus.

God showed me He had been preparing me for that particular experience for 20 years by giving me the same vision I had seen 20 years earlier while I was a very young pastor's wife. I saw those black children with eager, hungry eyes, and they were pulling on my skirt, just as in the first vision. For 20 years I had thought those black children were in Africa!

In a narrow, stinking, rat-infested alley of an over-populated Panamanian city, it happened just the way I had seen in my visions. Children came from every direction to the only playground they knew, the alley. I couldn't speak one word of their language nor they mine, but one of God's "coincidences" (a small miracle where God chooses to remain anonymous) happened. An 11-year-old Panamanian girl who had been raised in New York came running up and offered to interpret for me.

This went on for 2 weeks, every morning in the alleys and every night in the theater where the crusade was going on in which our youth were involved. My little interpreter returned to New York the day before we left. If that isn't God's timing!

That climaxed my work with children as a major effort, but God has led me to several other interests—Women's Ministries, writing, missions endeavors, and now working with single young women. You may not feel your life will ever be dramatic or adventuresome, but I have a motto: "Do what you can do and you will be surprised what you can do!"

The whole process is in your hands. God never forces His will on an unwilling person. I'm afraid we all fail to cooperate fully with God's will. But we should be able to say, "Hey, I'm doing better today than I did yesterday in seeking, finding, and doing God's will."

Here are some basic conditions that must be met. You cannot find God's will if . . .

There is sin in your heart.

You hang on to unyielded rights (total submission is required).

There's something yet undone that He has already told you to do.

The final decision regarding the will of God in your life must be your own. It is only the seeking mind and willing heart that can know the will of God.

Obedience today will bring guidance tomorrow. In finding God's will the only part of the game "Hide and Seek" you should play is, "Here I come with both eyes open!"

Fill in your own calendar and mark your "red-letter" day when there is no doubt in your mind about being in the will of God.

Chapter Four

# GENES AND GENDER

So far you have been exposed to some important choices for your life: to be or not to be a Christian; to get in or to get out of the church; to hide from or to seek God's will.

Other decisions you will face in the next few years concern your life-style, education, career, and love relationships, to name a few. But for now, the topic is YOU.

What could be more important? Take a short pause, a deep breath, and a long look at yourself. Do you like what you see? Who are you? How about your self-esteem? Are you totally pleased with your looks? How much is within your control?

Just what, for you, did genes and gender render?

Gender is simply the quality of being of the male or female sex. Human genetics is another story. In short, genes are what you inherit from the "family tree." Genes are the basic units of heredity. They are carried on the chromosomes of reproductive cells and transmit specific characteristics from parents to offspring. In biology class you may be taught all of this but you won't learn how to deal with your inheritance.

So, here you are, up a tree—the "family tree"— with the "trunk" (body) of Grandma, the "limbs" (arms or hands) of Dad, the "foliage" (hair) of Mom, and the "blossoms" (smile and beauty or lack of it) of Aunt Jane.

What do you do now?

First, come down out of the tree. The truth is *you are you*, in spite of certain things you have inherited, such as your coloring, bone structure, and height. "Each of us has about 50,000 genes. On the average, five or six are defective," reports the chairman of the Genetics Study Section of the National Institutes of Health. This same researcher says each person gets two copies of every gene; one from each parent. So you do have reason to look or act like one parent or both.

But I don't think our inherited traits leave us helpless to change. There are psychologists who disagree

and say, "A human being is born with spark, vitality, drive—call it what you will—or else he's born without it. If he hasn't got it, you can't spoon it into him." I say everyone gets a chance in the genetic lottery, true, but everyone also gets a chance to make changes in some areas.

BORROWED, BLUE EYES, AND TWO DIMPLES!

Every person, like every snowflake, is different. So what if you have your dad's blue eyes and your mom's dimples? You are an original. It's important you accept the way you were born—with a prominent nose, oversized ears, or whatever it is you dislike—if it's unchangeable.

You may feel you aren't blessed with many attri-

butes. Start with what you have. You probably have at least a dozen good features.

There are only 12 notes in the musical scale. Hundreds of thousands of unique and melodious tunes have been created with those 12 notes. You too can compose your own song—with intervals of semitones, sometimes minor notes, and quite frequently modulations, changes from one key to another. You may have to practice long and painfully before you can play the triumphant symphony of self-acceptance. But every song, in its distinctness, is a new creation—a new you.

As you ascend and descend life's scale and begin to combine your small handful of "notes" with the right rhythm and strokes, it will be your song. Bar after bar you can create, from what you have, a song of harmony, mellow, soft, and sweet, and all your own.

You have to decide to either live with yourself as you are, or begin to make some changes now, to be happy. The choice is yours. Write your own music.

The other day I noticed the most vibrant high school girl talking with her mother, as friends would talk. I decided to find out why she was so jubilant. She didn't act displeased with herself at all. I wanted to know if she had reason to be. She consented to this short interview.

*Are you pleased with your looks?*

"Yes, I am," she answered quickly. "I just got my braces off my teeth today. I got my hair cut and I've lost 25 pounds."

I could see why she would be pleased! What an improvement program she had been through. She went ahead to tell me, voluntarily, that she knew she would never be "the perfect me—my dream" but she was working on it. She said, "I weighed 115 pounds in the third grade, so my weight problem started early."

*Do you have inherited characteristics?*

"My dad's feet and my mom's legs." She laughed and commented, "My feet are ugly and I have big legs, but it doesn't bother me."

*Do you ever feel you want to "be me"?*

"Yeah," she said rather quietly, nodding her head.

*What would you change if you could?*

"My legs."

So it did bother her, but she refused to tolerate heredity ruling or ruining her life.

*How's your self-esteem?*

"When I'm with the 'up' group I want to be like them, but they're beginning to accept me like I am, and that helps me a lot to like myself. At first it wasn't that way. I have a good relationship with my mom and that helps too. My parents are divorced. My mom understands that when I feel like being alone, she should let me, and when I feel a need to go with friends, she allows this too. So all in all I don't have any problems *now* with myself."

We both were in a hurry so I closed the conversation with a promise we would get together again. I marvelled at this tall, thin, lovely young "remodeled" specimen of a do-it-yourselfer. She also shared her ideas about not marrying young, getting the education she wanted, and settling on a college. I found it hard to believe she was only 14 years old!

## FUN HOUSE MIRROR

You may not feel carefree. You may even be among those who do not have a good mental image of themselves. Or, your self-image may be far from right. There's something about seeing ourselves as we actually are that gets "out of whack"—like viewing yourself in the crazy mirror at the "fun house." This discrepancy works on a physical level too. It's the chubby girls who usually buy too-tight clothes and the willowy ones who consistently choose garments that are too big. It's the beauty who's convinced she's plain and the unattractive person who mentally endows herself with glamor.

"People can be quite wonderful, but often they're the very ones who feel miserable about themselves. The image usually has little to do with reality," says a Manhattan psychotherapist who regularly sees clients struggling with image problems.

It's neither healthy nor profitable to maintain a distorted image of yourself, whether that image is unrealistically high or unrealistically low. Neither the way others see you nor the way you see yourself is quite you! The pictures we get of ourselves are reflected by cloudy mirrors at best and often distorted. But if you are honest and concerned enough to get an accurate view of yourself, you have a launching pad to a new you, a new life, and a new world!

# PAIN BEING YOURSELF

Get to know yourself as you really are, complete with your strengths and your weaknesses. What is your disposition? your makeup? Do you think you're lousy? How about self-doubts? You're not alone. Everyone has them.

Don't forget, you are your own special self. If you have trouble accepting yourself, start your self-improvement plan. Set realistic goals for yourself. Make a checklist to see if you are spending enough time to keep yourself in order. Sloppiness, an unclean body, limp hair, and broken nails will never be the best you.

You must like yourself to be your best. To like yourself you must know your real self. What makes you "tick"? To discover your real self keep a record of a few things you do habitually. It may be painful, but you will know yourself much better. Chances are when you do get acquainted with yourself, you'll stop putting yourself down.

Here's a couple of good ideas to start your own personal-awareness campaign. Do this for 1 week.

1. Keep a record of your final thoughts before you go to sleep at night.

2. Keep a record of your spare time, and what you do when you have a choice.

3. Keep a record of what you read. Is it balanced, acceptable, spiritually stimulating, uplifting?

PUT DOWNS AND PUSH UPS

You may, unconsciously, be your own enemy because it's easy to ignore your strengths and pay special attention to your failures. This is putting yourself down. Others are guilty too. A put-down can be a look, a word, or a gesture. But you know, because you feel more worthless with each "knock."

Who among us is worthy? We stand perfected only in Christ's righteousness. To God, each of us is of great worth, and His evaluation is the one that counts.

To counter your put-downs, try doing mental pushups. Begin with yourself—evaluation, new ideas, self-helps. As in physical exercise, your pushups will become easier and you will get stronger with practice.

So what makes you what you are? Genes, gender, traits, grooming, self-acceptance, put-downs, pushups, worth? Yes, all of these and more. More, because *you* and Christ are at the top of the list.

*"But thou, O Lord, art a shield for me; my glory, and the lifter up of mine head"* (Psalm 3:3).

GETTING TO KNOW YOURSELF!

♪ LORD, THANK YOU FOR WHAT I AM! HELP ME TO ACCEPT WHAT I CANNOT CHANGE, AND TO MAKE THE CHANGES THAT NEED TO BE MADE TO BRING ABOUT PERFECT HARMONY WITHIN MYSELF AND WITH THEE...

AMEN. ♪♪

# Chapter Five

Groundwork has been laid for making friends, something everybody wants and everybody needs. How nice to know you have the freedom to choose your own special friends. But it isn't *all* wrapped up in the choosing.

*Do* you choose your friends? or do they choose you? Do your friendships just happen? It sounds simple, doesn't it? But lasting and meaningful friendships have to be developed very carefully.

A lot is being said today about interrelations— mutual or reciprocal relations. Reciprocal means "done or given by each of two to the other." Many lonely people—maybe some girls you know, or *you*—fail to do their share of giving to the other.

There are more and more people doing their own thing. Haven't you heard, "If they like me they like me. If they don't, they don't"? "They" meaning any-body that these people who are doing their own thing want it to mean. These people act as if they really don't care whether they have friends or not. It's a front. How lonely the hour must be when they have to sit quietly by themselves somewhere.

## A Girl's Best Friend

As you've grown up you may have dropped "best"

friend from your vocabulary. In early childhood it is always a "best" and a "worst" friend who can be switched or replaced within the hour. You may call your special friend a good friend or introduce her as "one of my close friends." Or perhaps she is your "best" friend. How fortunate you are if you have one.

We like to think we have a lot of friends. The term *friend* is used loosely. If I were to ask you about yours you might start listing acquaintances whom you invite to parties and play tennis, converse, and eat with. These may be people you know personally and for whom you have warm regard. But all of these "chums" or "pals" do not make it to the top of the close bosom-friend list. Special close friends are rare and invaluable. Rare, because they are so hard to find and invaluable because they contribute so much of genuine value to your life.

A close friend believes in you, stands up for you, and understands you. A close friend may understand you better than you understand yourself. Trust is a big word in close friendships.

One writer interprets friendship as: "The feeling you possess for a particular person as distinct from all other persons. It is a very beautiful and intimate and close relationship which is destroyed if it is bestowed casually." Women feel differently than men about the meaning of friendship. A British sociologist found in a recent study that women felt trust and confidentiality were more important while men emphasized the pleasure they found in a friend's company.

Who needs friends? Each of us does. The best therapy in the world when you feel threatened at the risk of being yourself, is to have a close friend with whom to share your feelings, your moods, and your ideas. A good friend will allow you to take your mask off and will leave your freedom intact; helping you be fully what you are and enhancing the qualities you have.

## LOOK WHO'S HERE...
### a friendly face!

Do you have to be friendly to make friends? God's Word gives a formula:

> A man that hath friends must show himself friendly: and there is a friend that sticketh closer than a brother (Proverbs 18:24).

Before we get too far from this verse of Scripture, have you tried Jesus for a friend? Jesus used the word *friend* a number of times. He said, "Greater love hath no man than this, that a man lay down his life for his friends" (John 15:13). He did that for us! Check out something else He said about friends in verses 14 and 15. A songwriter penned and recorded the words, "Not just servants, but we're friends . . . ," taken from the 15th verse.

At the time of this new song I was feeling so indebted to Jesus. I was struggling to do more projects and more committee work to repay Christ. When I realized He wants us for a friend that changed the picture. A friend will do whatever needs doing for another friend and I continue to, but not out of servitude, out of friendship. I find others, to my distress, who do not know about or accept His friendship. He wants to be your friend. After you receive Jesus as a friend then you will "come on" to your earthly friends in a perceptive and more appreciative way.

How do you approach your colleagues? with a smile, a nod, a wave? or a frown, a cold shoulder, a slight disregard of their presence? It's that first impression that stays with a person the longest. There's an adage that goes, "The smile on your face is the light in the window that tells people that you are at home." In making friends this is one area you can master. It is worth a try. Smile.

## CLICK! GET IN THE PICTURE!

The attraction two people sometimes experience at a first meeting—chemistry or vibrations, call it what you wish—is the "makings" of a lasting friendship. The elements are there but they have to be processed correctly. A little later we'll talk about developing and processing friendship. First let's talk about getting in the picture.

Some friends came to be my close friends because I befriended them, and others, because they befriended me. When a friendship begins to come into focus you have to decide if you want "in" the picture.

There are short-term and long-term friends. Unavoidable circumstances sometimes cut a friendship short, but often it's a lack of action that keeps it from developing.

One of my close friends, Clara, is blind. I met her a few years ago before her third child was born. Clara's husband is also blind. Their three children have normal sight and are beautiful. I went to the hospital with Clara and stayed with her when the baby came. In gratitude she named the baby after our daughter.

I used to sit in amazement watching Clara put away her groceries; cans of beans in line, cans of corn in stacks. She bought her groceries systematically and her system carried over at home. I would go home from her house, close my eyes tightly, and try to do the things we take for granted with eyesight. It was alarming to me how I stumbled around!

The first time I had Clara's family over for dinner I could hardly eat because I felt so sorry for my sightless friends, but I soon learned they were far too efficient for pity! We live in different states now but Clara calls me every year on my birthday. We enjoy talking as much as ever. She is a long-term friend and grows dearer as the years pass.

In Dar es Salaam, the enchanting oceanfront capital city of Tanzania, East Africa, I made several short-term friends and a few lasting friendships. Nostalgia nags me as I pull my scrapbook out and recall the visit.

Dar es Salaam ("Haven of Peace") is one of the most informal and relaxed capitals in the world.

*Dear Dar: I found infinite charm in*
*your palm-fringed harbor, busy with shipping—*
*Your silver-sanded beaches, washed by the*
*warm waters of the Indian Ocean—*
*Your craftsmen practicing their skills—*
*Your bustling colorful city—*
*But in my memory your gentle and kind*
*people mean more!*

A little African girl insisted I wait for her while she breathlessly ran to her apartment and brought back a tiny faded black-and-white photograph of a giraffe. In the far distance was a tall mountain. I assumed it was Mt. Kilimanjaro, the highest in Africa (over 19,000 feet high). When we flew over it coming from Nairobi I wasn't up to taking pictures. The African pilot had tilted the plane too close to the mountain for me! The picture was the little girl's prized possession. She wanted me to have it. We were friends. Remembering, I have deep emotions.

DO YOUR OWN DEVELOPING

Let's compare friendships to photography. The

49

camera is loaded with film—undeveloped friendships. Your friendships are significant. Your friends are important. They hold a power of influence over you in many areas of your life. Even the giraffe, in my gift photo from Africa, had enough sense to get in the picture with something of prominence.

But there's more to a photo than a print. There's more to a friend than a snapshot. The camera, photographer, film, lighting, posing, exposing, and developing all make a good photograph. Many things go into producing a good friendship too.

Snap, click! What happens after you take a roll of film? Your camera then contains a series of exposed latent images ready for development; ready to be treated. But actually they are nothing worthwhile until they are developed into a contact sheet of negatives to be retouched and enlarged.

At the beginning of a friendship, when you've been introduced to a likely candidate, there may be no apparent material for bringing the friendship into existence—an unrevealed roll of exposed film. So, if you want to develop the friendship it must go through a certain processing.

First, film has to be processed in a darkroom, or in a daylight developing tank, in total darkness. New friendships are like that. You are in the dark. You know nothing about the new friend. Will you like the things she does? Will she agree with you? You can't see yet what it will turn into or what your friend will think of you. It takes a certain timing, like the stages of developing film.

A full-blown friendship will emerge if you keep the action going. Don't stop in the middle of the processing. Call a friend. Get better acquainted. Go out of your way to do something you know would please your friend. Get together. Do things you both enjoy.

Several years ago we had a teenager from out of town visiting in our home. I discovered she had many of the same interests I had, including writing. We kept in touch even though there was an age difference between us. It never seemed to matter. On occasion I sent her magazines and books marked especially for her that I thought would help. And she soon was published. It became a bond between us; a step in the developing. We are the closest of friends to this day. She confides in me by long-distance telephone and I'm always overjoyed when on rare occasions we can get together. It takes such a little effort to develop a really beautiful friendship.

There may be old friends that could and should have a second chance to get in the picture with you. It's nice to insist on a "double exposure" once in a while. Double exposure means exposing the same film twice. Ordinarily this is shunned by photographers, except, that is, for special effect. This composite (or two subjects on one frame of film) can be done by special developing. What could bring more joy than two friends in the same frame of film . . . and in the same frame of mind?

# How to treat a friend.

## DOs

**1**

Be a good listener (means giving yourself unselfishly to people and what concerns them. Listen with your ears, mind, and heart)

**2**

Express and share emotions

**3**

Treat with kindness and respect

**4**

Befriend a few winners (those who stay on top)

**5**

Guard your friendships

## DON'Ts

**1**

Avoid cliquishness (using unity of a few friendships to crowd out competition of others)

**2**

Don't intentionally hurt (if you do, apologize)

**3**

Don't look for faults

**4**

Don't *over*give advice (but one who *never* gives advice usually doubts her own opinion, is fearful of the outcome, and operates defensively)

## Chapter Six

Where the ACTION is.

Adolescence, the period of growth from puberty to adulthood, is a painful, self-doubting time of adjustment. The best and the worst emerge from the same person, namely you. Body changes create some bewilderment. Pent-up emotions have to be unloosed, in one way or another. Personalities are still in the mold.

Consequently, you act and react in ways you like and dislike all at the same time. It's a guessing game to see what each day brings to you and what each day has to take from you. As Christians we're committed to face squarely some issues of our lives; bridging the gap of frail human behavior in the natural and the Christian view.

There are people who automatically bring out in you the highest qualities you possess simply by understanding why you do what you do and act the way you act. When they believe in you and sincerely regard your pursuit of the moment worthy and worthwhile, it's like setting off a reverberation. You go from okay to good, from good to better, from better to excellent, and from excellent to best performance.

A warden of a federal house of detention said: "If you treat an individual as he is, he'll stay as he is. But if you treat him as if he were what he ought to be or could be, perhaps he will become that." I've heard most of my life, "Treat a girl like a queen, and she'll act like a queen." You may be thinking, "But nobody treats me like a queen."

What about all those people—a much higher percentage—who do not care enough to set you in motion? How do you react to a jeer? a rejection? a defeat? Do you rebel at authority? Are you ever a snob? Are you jealous? These are behavior defects that harass you off and on, aren't they?

Your choice is not between being the worst person that ever lived and being perfect. Your choice is finding out about your behavior patterns in general and making sure that the action is where it should be. You can't give the answer before the question is asked. What are your good responses and your inconsistencies; the positives and the negatives of your everyday living? A realistic goal is to act in a way that you will be proud to continue into adulthood.

What you *think* you are is not really that important. It's true we all tend to take our imperfections too seriously. It's kind of a reverse vanity. We assume everyone is paying attention to every detail, each movement, each intonation of our voice, when actually people seldom notice what we're doing. The important thing is what you do with what you are. How you behave and why.

# Inconsistencies
## of
## Teenagers

### How do you measure up?

✓

☑ HATES RIGID RULES & HAVING TO CONFORM.

✓

☐ CONFORMS IN EVERY WAY TO PEERS: IN DRESS, IDEAS, MUSIC & ENTERTAINMENT.

— 1 —

☐ REJECTS UNDUE REGARD FOR MATERIAL SIDE OF LIFE.

☐ "DROOLS" OVER HIGHEST PRICED SHOES IN STORE WINDOW.

— 2 —

☐ HAPPY, CHEERFUL, LAUGHING.

☐ MELANCHOLY & MOODY.

☐ SPURNS AUTHORITY.

— 3 —

☐ ACCEPTS AS "LAW AND GOSPEL" FROM FAVORITE IDOL.

"If you could kick the person responsible for most of your problems, you would not be able to sit down for 6 months!"

That may sound a little humorous to you, but don't

you agree? Most of us, at one time or another, have done things we are not very proud of later on. It may seem to be the right thing to do at the time, but later when you get caught, or even if you don't, you feel it wasn't so "cool" after all.

A girl I know was told by her parents not to leave a basketball game before it was over. Since she had not been driving very long her dad was uneasy about her having the car. Contrary to her parents' request she decided to leave early anyway with some of her friends. Just as she drove away, a boy she had previously dated pulled in front of her car sharply, causing her to hit a post, run the car along a wire, and flip it on its side. In an instant she was caught. Her parents had to be called. It was a bad scene, although no one was injured. She could hardly face her parents because of the hurt she had caused them. The wrecked car was a haunting reminder.

This was not her normal behavior. Her mom and dad were good Christian parents and even though she had reacted unwisely in a critical moment they knew it was not like her. She had already proved herself to be trustworthy in other matters. Therefore, she got consideration and support from her parents. This is good when a young person earns it. A mistake once in a while can be overlooked if it is not routine behavior.

This family handled the crisis so beautifully. In a final attempt to lift the daughter out of her despondency her dad took her out of town for dinner one evening without the other family members. It worked wonders. She held her head high again and began to act a little like a queen!

She could have had the attitude, "I goofed! No one trusts me, I may as well do my own thing." Rebellion could have set in.

*Rebellion* is one of the uglier words connected with antisocial behavior. It is a negative reaction that will produce defeat to a Christian every time. It is resistance to authority; active opposition. Read how Saul disobeyed God, and Samuel, after praying all night for him, told him: "To obey is better than sacrifice. . . . For rebellion is as the sin of witchcraft, and stubbornness is as iniquity and idolatry" (1 Samuel 15:22, 23).

The way you act and react, your responses, your emotions, your manner of conducting yourself under given circumstances—your whole behavior pattern is where the action is. Take a moment to take a serious look. It may well pull you right out of a pack of trouble. I hope so.

Jesus allows us the freedom to be human beings. The maturing person must begin to establish some form of independence, but why does it have to be a civil war? I've always wondered, if the parents want the child to grow up and the child is ready to grow up, why the hassle? I think it is because the maturing process is not defined. Parents don't teach responsibility and youth shun it.

When you are given responsibility—something you are answerable for, an obligation you are to meet—see that you finish the task. You'll never be able to act without superior authority unless you learn to be dependable.

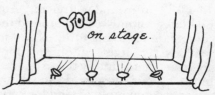

Responsibility is simply accountability for one's

actions. No longer should you shift the blame or claim innocence in situations where you are in the wrong. The most evident proof of maturity is accepting something exactly as it is. If you are on the stage in full drama don't pretend you are the prop man behind the scene or the make-up girl instead of the actress. Facing the charges is growing up. This kind of growth comes from within.

A complaint I hear a lot from teenagers is, "My parents treat me like a baby!" I have observed in some cases it is "act like a baby . . . treat like a baby."

Why don't you attempt to act very grown up and see if you gain any ground in esteem and courtesy from others? Accept every ounce of responsibility that's rightfully yours. Accept your share of the load of chores that pile up around your home. Admit your share of the blame for messes left around the house. Take on your share in saving utilities and not being wasteful with water, lights, fuel, and food. It's a throw-away society and cutting down on waste won't be easy, but it is your place to do so.

You alone are accountable to God for your dedication. You are liable for your Bible study. There are all kinds of responsibilities and you won't have much trouble detecting what part you *should* take. Doing what you know to do is the problem.

> Therefore to him that knoweth to do good, and doeth it not, to him it is sin (James 4:17).

# BLUNDMRS?
### ...TAKE ACTION!

You, in your youth, have far too much to offer the Christian community to allow a few behavior flaws to foul up your testimony. You may be tempted to throw out Christianity as a legitimate option because you're not a good Christian example all the time. Believe me there's a better solution. You do not have to change, grow, or be good to acquire God's love. Rather, you are loved so you can change, grow, and be good.

When you get to the place where you can operate in God's love; when He fills you to the brim with the Holy Spirit; people won't have to be making allowances for you. Do you hear remarks such as these?

"She's moody. Don't let what she says get to you." "She's sort of sensitive. Better not bring up that subject."

When you are tactless are you guilty of a cop-out? Do you tell your friends, "I always say what I think! Tough on you if you can't accept honesty!" Some of the assertiveness teaching going around is contrary to Christian behavior. There is never an excuse to be rude or offensive. Express your opinion in love and gentleness.

Do you hurt others by telling lies? Do you give teachers or parents a hard time? If you have these faults you should want to change. You must want to want to. You must want to even when you don't want to!

The Scriptures are full of the failures of God's children. Very few, if any, of them lived a consistent life of victory, free of all turmoil or attacks from Satan. God never threw them out. His love was always so near they were able to function until victory came again.

Simon Peter, for example, was a pretty weak, unstable character. He was extremely hotheaded. Jesus could have wished it were not a known fact that Peter was one of His followers when Peter flew into a rage and cut off the ear of the high priest's servant, or when he denied he was a friend of Jesus when the whole city knew he was one of the bunch. Do you know how Jesus handled Peter? In a loving, patient way. At one point Jesus told him He had prayed for him.

> And the Lord said, Simon, Simon, behold, Satan hath desired to have you, that he may sift you as wheat: but I have prayed for thee, that thy faith fail not (Luke 22:31, 32).

Peter finally became one of Christ's most effective workers.

What matters to Jesus is not that you do all the wrong things, but that you come to Him honestly with your mistakes and confess them, asking forgiveness. As you do this He can teach you through your blunders!

*I am persuaded, that neither disobedience, nor rebellion, nor screamings, nor sarcasms, nor present phobias, nor insecurities to come, nor exaggerations, nor procrastinations nor any other unacceptable anti-social behavior, shall be able to separate me from the love of God, which is in Christ Jesus our Lord.*

*Because...*

"In all these things we are more than conquerers through him that loved us" (Romans 8:37).

# Chapter Seven

Before we get into this chapter on dating, how about taking a backward glance at some of the lessons you have learned?

Chapter 1 got you started on the right track; leaving your guilt pack—whatever sins you were carrying around—at the Cross.

Chapter 2 should have helped you locate a certain spot in your church for you to serve, after you killed the spider, which represented your fears.

The third chapter, on finding God's will, overlaps all the other chapters. God's Word is "a lamp unto [your] feet, and a light unto [your] path" (Psalm 119:105) and reveals His will for you a step at a time. As you follow His revealed will, the hidden comes to light. You are a well-adjusted young Christian if you are seeking His will in every aspect of your life. We can't play games with God.

In the fourth chapter you decided to accept your lot, the unchangeables in yourself. Didn't you? You also saw that the choice is yours to make *some* changes and how you can write your own music.

"Double Exposure" put you in the picture with your friends and hopefully helped you learn how to develop your friendships.

The last chapter dealt with the way you act and react—your behavior; both acceptable and unacceptable. So you should be acting like an angel this

week! This puts you in the frame of mind to be able to make decent judgments about dating. Then there are no problems? Ohhh! I can hear the groans.

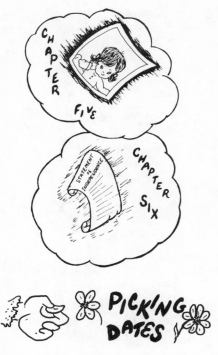

## PICKING DATES

Christian girls do have their own set of problems built in; wanting to date only Christian boys. The only way to find a spiritual Christian to date is to be one. If Christ is the center of your life then all your decisions must cluster around Him. That takes in dating and your relationships with the opposite sex.

Christ doesn't get to go on many dates but you could invite Him along on yours. Doing things the Christian way makes life a lot simpler. It means choosing carefully what you say, what you do, and where you go. If you are the right kind of person you're going to attract the right kind of boys.

The Bible does not positively forbid dating non-Christians but there are passages forbidding heavy association with the unbeliever. (Check 2 Corinthians 6:14, 17, 18.) Excuses you might give for going out with non-Christians have holes in them, besides the risks.

**Excuse:** "I want to witness to him."

Great soul winners will tell you witnessing is difficult when the person is close to you emotionally.

**Excuse:** "I didn't know he wasn't a Christian."

If you don't know him very well this could be the case, but you should have an understanding. Be brave about dating on your terms. Invite him over to your house to get acquainted. Discuss your beliefs. If it scares him off, the better for you. If he is a true believer he will be glad to have a Christian girl.

How do most girls in your school go about picking someone to date? What generally are they looking for? the football hero? an escort? a companion? a friend? a lover? the most popular boy in class? Do girls go out with anyone who asks them? should *you*?

Girls have the disadvantage in picking dates. It is usually the boy, as you well know, who gets to do the picking, but you do get to say yes or no. Boys wonder if they will be turned down. They say the girl has the advantage.

When you make a definite commitment not to date non-Christians, stick to it. If you know the boy quite well and don't know if he's a Christian or not, most likely he isn't. To meet boys who are Christ-centered, go where they hang out. You won't find them at a dance or other questionable places. If you go out with certain types, you will be classified with them.

Retreats, youth services, conferences, conventions, and rallies are ideal places to meet Christians. Of course, your own church should be attended faithfully. You never know when a new face will show, if you are not completely sold on dating the regular guys in your church. It is often like dating your brother, you are so close to them.

# DADS ARE LIKE THAT!

I guess the biggest problem when you start dating is parents—aside from finding a boy with the same Christian standards who is available and wants to date you.

When our daughter started dating she was a typical on-the-go modern Christian teenager. Her dad was a typical stay-at-home, "old-fashioned," nearing-middle-age, Christian father.

Her first date alone with a young man couldn't have been with a longtime friend, the kid down the street, or a boy from our local church. No, none of those would have caused a battle line to be drawn so quickly. Her date, a young man 3 years her senior, drove in from another state and swooped her off into the night in a fast-moving automobile. Meanwhile, her dad—after the first hour—paced the floor and alternately looked at his watch and out the front door.

"He is a good-looking young man, isn't he?" I ventured. My husband nodded.

"He's nice," I tried again. My husband nodded.

"We didn't tell her what time to be in," he finally muttered. Well, he wasn't stricken dumb after all!

They had met at a national church convention in Kansas City. He was from Missouri; we were from Texas. Who would have thought we'd ever see him again? But evidently they got pretty well acquainted. Letters were crossing in the mail when we got home.

Then "out of the blue" (to us anyway—we've always thought our daughter knew all along), this young man called and said he was in the state with a pastor friend and family and was coming to a town not far from where we lived. Could he come over and take her out to dinner?

What could we say? Oh, there's much we *could* have said but what we did say was, "Sure. How nice of him to ask you." It might have been because we were pastors and wondered what the pastor friend would think if we refused, or because we halfway trusted the boy, or because we were caught off guard. Whatever the reason, it was all arranged before we had time to think about it.

With them gone we had time to think about it. Back to the pacing. That was a side of my husband I had never seen. Before long he blurted out, "What could they possibly be doing for an hour and a half?"

I lost track of time after that. It must have been a whole 20 or 30 minutes before we heard our daughter's sharp little giggle outside the window. They briefed us on the new boy friend's initiation to Texas food, then headed for the music room. The rest of the evening went beautifully. We popped in every once in a while. Their music and singing floated through the house.

Our "old-fashioned," middle-aged dad turned into a modern, rather young, distinguished, jolly good father! What brought about the reaction and then the change?

## BATTLE LINES

There is one thing that all dads seem to have in common. When it comes to their daughters it's a duel over who is the most capable of protecting and shielding the little princess.

It wasn't much different when I grew up and probably won't be too much different when your children grow up. Dads are dads and they each have their own way of expressing approval and disapproval of "dates."

My parents married young. My dad went into the army when I was a teenager. My first date after we moved from Lubbock and followed him to the army camp in Louisiana was a disaster.

I met a new boy on the bus. He asked me one Friday just before I got off the bus if he could take me to a family party. I knew he was a Christian even though I didn't know him very well. We had shared a meal with some others and he had been asked to offer thanks for the food. I waved with a smile and nodded "yes" as I got off the bus.

On a one-to-one basis this was my first date and I had made it without consulting my parents. I confided in my mother as soon as I got home, but my father was not a Christian and he seemed to judge everyone by himself. One thing, he was not about to let my dating get kicked off with a Louisiana Cajun.

When the young man came to pick me up in his folk's car and bounced up to the door, I backed away. Dad was between us. I heard him say very sternly, "No, I guess she'd better walk with us."

I was embarrassed and awkward and all those good things, but I survived. My new beau came to my rescue.

"That's fine," he said, "I'll just walk with you." So we walked nearly a mile through the heavy wooded area to the neighbor's house for the party. My parents strolled along within hearing distance and my little 3-year-old brother, dressed in an exact copy of Dad's army suit, cap, stripes, and all, tagged along between us holding my fellow's hand!

## Going -Going -Gone!

If it weren't for parents and curfews, dating would be so much more fun! Have you ever thought that? But together parents and curfews make quite a team *for* you, not against you.

Time has a way of being swallowed up with each bite of pizza—and that's pretty fast. When your time to be home starts looming up in front of you with every bat of your eye, it makes you wonder who ever invented curfews and why.

Curfews are rules for your own good, as most rules are. Have you ever thought of them this way?

*Curfews* let me know someone cares enough to watch out for my welfare.

*Curfews* help me discipline myself.

*Curfews* say, "Hey, I have rules I must abide by. I have to answer to my parents because I love them and they love me."

*Curfews* keep me off the streets during unsafe hours.

*Curfews* help me get the rest I need.

*Curfews* give me a chance to prove myself dependable.

The list could go on and on. Add to it if you want to and thank God for your curfews.

To get more freedom from your parents, be courteous enough to call them when an unavoidable delay keeps you from getting home on time.

Dating can be a fun-filled, pleasure-packed joy-ride, but you can have just as much fun if you don't have a date. About the only thing you will miss by going in a crowd "dateless" is a reckless ride home and a goodnight peck-of-a-kiss. You can live without both.

## Chapter Eight

# Everybody's Doing It!

This subject may appear to be a continuation of "Where the Action Is"—the way you act and react. But it will also embrace your values, your standards, and your ideals in action—your Christian conduct.

Tons could be written on teenage misconduct, immorality, drugs, pregnancies, and abortions, which are so prevalent today. This side of the picture hurts and is a shame to our society. But, more than that, the shame envelops the young people involved and they hurt. I'd like to put a Band-Aid on every aching heart. But the best I can do is pen words and pray the message gets through.

The Bible does not dodge the issue. It says the basic problems of society are within man himself. Every person has good and bad in him. Because God has given us freedom, every person has the same problem. This freedom meets its most rigid test when you decide which to let be dominant—the *natural man* or the *spiritual man*. There are two sides and you do the choosing.

## Choosing Sides

Paul calls the two sides of the human personality "flesh" and "spirit." By flesh he means the impulses we have that are not good. He is talking about man's

"Won't you come share with me.... it's so much nicer here!"

FRUIT of the SPIRIT

WORKS OF THE FLESH

inner self, not his body. These two, "flesh" and "spirit," wage war against one another during your whole Christian life. The battleground is you! When the battle gets vigorous, remember, Christ has done His part, you must do yours.

These two sides are found in Galatians 5:19-23. *Today's English Version* lists the works of the flesh and the fruit (or harvest) of the Spirit in understandable terms:

| *Flesh* | *Spirit* |
|---|---|
| hostility | peace |
| jealousy | joy |
| envy | love |
| anger | kindness |
| indecency | goodness |
| immorality | faithfulness |
| idolatry | humility |
| ambition | patience |
| drunkenness | self-control |

*The Living Bible* makes it really clear:

But when you follow your own wrong inclinations your lives will produce these evil results: impure thoughts, eagerness for lustful pleasure, idolatry, spiritism (that is, encouraging the activity of demons), hatred and fighting, jealousy and anger, constant effort to get the best for yourself, complaints and criticisms, the feeling that everyone else is wrong except those in your own little group—and there will be wrong doctrine, envy, murder, drunkenness, wild parties, and all that sort of thing. Let me tell you again as I have before, that anyone living that sort of life will not inherit the kingdom of God.

The fruit of the Spirit is the Biblical description of a mature Christian. If, after you look over the works of the flesh, you discover you are on that side dillydallying around, you either haven't changed sides or you are a guest on enemy territory. Your conduct is the cart that carries you *from* one side *to* the other.

Growing Christians go through a *from-to* process. They go from one pattern of attitudes and conduct to the other side. Paul did not hound the Christians to

change from one column to the other column. He knew this was not possible by one's own efforts. The Holy Spirit must be allowed to pull your conduct cart from one side to the other. It is a must to be "*led* by the Spirit."

Read the words Paul wrote to the Christians of his day in the verses preceding the two lists. In Galatians 5:16-18 he says because the flesh and Spirit are contrary to each other, you cannot do the things you want to do. Paul says: "I advise you to obey only the Holy Spirit's instructions. He will tell you where to go and what to do, and then you won't always be doing the wrong things your evil nature wants you to" (Galatians 5:16, *The Living Bible*).

# SELF-CHOSEN STANDARDS

Take a closer look at your values, morals, and self-chosen standards of conduct. Who's in control? What are some things that make you feel better about yourself? Why don't you write down everything you can think of? Finding the things that help you feel good about yourself may be a real challenge.

Since you've changed sides, go down the list of the

fruit of the Spirit. What conduct have you displayed lately that gave you *peace*? Was it overlooking your sister's hatefulness instead of becoming hostile? Did some of your ideals in action bring you *joy*? So what if your best girl friend won "Miss Personality" at youth camp. You were happy, not jealous.

Let's continue down the list. When did you last overflow with *love* for someone? Write the last act of *kindness* you actually performed. All these acts have proved your *faithfulness*, right? You don't feel one bit haughty about what you are doing so there's *humility*. Patience and self-control may be something else! Can you honestly confirm these two by writing down the last time you bit your lip or tongue while your patience suffered long? In the raging battle did *self-control* win triumphantly? Write about the experience in detail. It will be a flag of victory for you or a guideline for the next time.

This, in writing, could be your code. Pin it up somewhere so you can see it often. Decorate it creatively, anyway you choose. If you were pleased or displeased, it will serve as a reminder of the standard you have set for yourself at this point in your life. And Christ and the Holy Spirit are right there to help and support you in holding that standard up.

You are a new creature in Christ. You don't have to keep acting like your old sinful self. True, it's an off-and-on battle, but you never have to lose.

# PASSPORT TO BELONGING

So everybody's doing it. Do you ever try to pull that on your parents? Or worse yet, on yourself? What is *it* that everybody's doing?

The statistics are grim when we review the teen scene. You are caught between your own high moral standards and the more liberal trends of our time. But you need not be confused. Respect is a better passport to belonging than conformity. Belonging where you really fit—without the farce of roleplaying.

Who needs fulfillment in drugs, alcohol, self-styled music freaks, or a sexual drive that leads to teen pregnancies, "runaways," and suicides? Certainly not the Christian young person.

DRUGS
ALCOHOL
FREAK·MUSIC
SEX ABUSE

Current estimates are that 600,000 to 1 million children run away from home annually. At least half are girls—many are no older than 13 or 14. According to one authority, only drug abuse is a bigger problem for adolescent Americans and their parents.

I heard about a teenage boy who wrote a crisis-line service. He realized not only his life, but also the lives of his entire generation, were in jeopardy by the tragic trap of drugs.

The young man was worried about the world when his generation has to take over. "Can you imagine a government of hopheads? surgeons who are stoned? You know it takes a lot of study to get to be a scientist.

I don't know anybody who wants to study that long," he said. Then he began to talk about the life he had gotten himself into by starting on drugs at an early age.

Most of the time he doesn't even go to school. All his friends are on drugs and don't want to do anything except "fly" as long as possible and then lay plans to get high again. More and more he finds himself not caring about anything. He said, "I know something is happening in my head." His friends don't bother to have parties or do any fun things anymore. None of them are in sports.

The saddest part of his story is his confession, "I don't think I could quit if I wanted to. It is the only friend that never lets me down." The truth is, he is being *dragged* down. Let down? Maybe not, but he is getting lower and lower with each trip.

Another major hurdle during this period of youth is the necessary adjustment to the powerful new sexual drive which the maturing person finds, at times, overwhelming. Ann Landers revealed this shocking statistic: over 17,000 babies were born to mothers under 14 years of age in 1 year!

## CRUTCHES ARE FOR CRIPPLES

As a Christian teen, you should guard this beautiful and natural instinct God has placed within you. The feeling and experience should be reserved for sharing with that very special person in your life—your marriage partner. To be able to do this, girls should be careful about wearing provocative clothing to attract male attention and should refrain from petting. Petting is touching and feeling during lovemaking, especially those parts of the body that are sensitive sexually. I doubt a definition is needed, but I have been asked, "Exactly what is petting?" Christian young singles should resist even "light" petting.

Masters and Johnson, a highly respected team of researchers on sexual functioning, were on a talk show I was watching. They talked with teenage girls in the audience. The question was asked, "How many of you have made love?" By the grins, nods, and reluctant show of hands, there were quite a few. "How many of you are emotionally ready for lovemaking?" was the next question. Only two hands were raised in a large room full of girls. Sex behavior appears to carry the biggest burden of guilt of all immoral conduct.

Only the crippled need crutches. None of these props or crutches—sex, drugs, alcohol, and freak music entertainers—holds a young person up very long.

The suicide rate among teens is frightening. Suicides and attempted suicides have increased 300 percent in the last 20 years among teenagers. More than 4,000 a year take this route.

Young people who have only their carnal nature to rely on are in trouble. But everyone is *not* doing it! The population in the United States has passed the 220-million mark and gains one more person every 19 seconds. There are people, and lots of them, who haven't bought disguised sin, sold under the brand names of "moral relativity" and "situational ethics."

So you see how it is: my new life tells me to do right, but the old nature that is still inside me loves to sin. Oh, what a terrible predicament I'm in! Who will free me from my slavery to this deadly lower nature? Thank God! It has been done by Jesus Christ our Lord. He has set me free (Romans 7:24, 25, *The Living Bible*).

Chapter Nine

# HEY! I'm HIRED!

Girls have a chance and a choice today, unlike any other time in history, for training and for job opportunities. Things have changed. Everybody's pulling for you! Or so it seems to me.

Progress reports from here and there—the U.S. Department of Labor (Employment Standards Administration, Women's Bureau, Washington, D.C.), "Project on Equal Education Rights," "Report on Women" from the U.S. Employment Service, and new laws—all say "good news for girls!"

Academic and vocational counselors I talked with indicated such exuberance and eagerness to share their piles of information and training programs with high school students. Personnel people spoke a good word for the high school girls working in all sorts of jobs. The few complaints voiced were logical and will be discussed later.

So, although it is quite natural for young people to get uptight at the very thought of a big scary boss and the competition in the workaday world, there's no real reason for fear. Yet, in rating their problems, students usually put "choosing a job" near or at the top of their list.

One report stated that during the decade 1965 to 1975, some 14 million additional jobs were developed in new or expanding industries. These new

jobs have provided employment opportunities for more than 9 million women.

Where do you find that one-in-9-million job that is right for you? After you've found it how do you get hired? Once you're hired, how do you keep the job? When you become secure in your work how do you advance? These questions jump to your mind, but the answers come more slowly.

Some of the programs offered in high school do all but put you on the job of your choice for life, or as long as you wish. But this training is sometimes rejected for lack of interest.

There's VOE (Vocational Office Education), DE (Distributive Education), ICT (Industrial Cooperative Training), HECE (Home Economics Co-op Education)—to name a few good training programs. I'd like to add one, WNT—Why Not Train! The co-op and multicampus programs are a definite advancement. The way I understand it, the co-op program combines—to the satisfaction of counselor, student, parent, and employer—training with the actual work schedule.

One distraught counselor went through the entire counseling procedure with me—middle school through the senior year. He said "interests tests" revealed no measurable results for a lot of the kids.

The college "major-minor finder" didn't work for all of them either. When a young person did show interest enough for a personal interview the counselor would follow it up. Maybe 2 years later the student would reply when asked about it, "I really haven't thought about it anymore." After all that! So what is being said is the same old formula, "Plan your work, and work your plan," to be successful.

### The WORKING WORLD

Counselors were careful to let me know no distinction is made between male and female in the educational or vocational programs. Congress passed a bill calling for an end to sex stereotyping in vocational education (September 19, 1976). To begin with, $50,000 of each state's federal allotment was set aside to hire full-time staff to help end sex bias in vocational education. That same month, first-year money awards for projects to end sex bias in education—totaling over $6.2 million in federal funds—were announced by the U.S. Office of Education. Since then opportunities have kept expanding for girls. Let's learn how to grasp at least one of those opportunities.

At the very outset of your breakaway into the working world, whether it is your first job or your sixth short-term experimental stint, before you go exploring too far, remember God is out there in the working world too. He still wants the best for you and wants your best for Him. Let that be a matter of prayer each day. What a difference it will make! To do your best for God, you should always be your best for your employer.

GOD'S BEST
↑↓↓↓↑
MY BEST

The earlier you begin asking God about *all* your decisions the sooner you will notice a sense of direction and an interest will take shape. You can build on that interest; God often allows you the desires of your heart. Until you make up your own mind about what type of job you want to prepare for no one else can give you much assistance. And there's tough competition, not only from male counterparts but also from each other. So, here are some tips.

APPLY! ALONE?!

Once you decide to apply for a certain job, gather everything you will need to answer the questions an employer may ask. You more than likely will be requested to fill out an application form asking about previous employment and schooling. References may be needed.

Take your own pen and have all information

readily available. Check with those persons whom you plan to give as references so as not to take them by surprise. Copy their names and addresses before you leave home so you will not have to ask for a telephone directory. Figure out the dates you worked at certain places before you get there. Be sure you know your social security number or have your card with you. These may seem to be small matters, but they can throw you into chaos if you don't go prepared.

You must go alone to approach an employer. Alone? Surely. And if you will think, you'll know why. He might suspect you are not mature enough for the job, or that you're sharing a brain, if you come with someone else. You have to convince him. In doing that, you should apply for a specific job and know something about the position you are applying for. If there is no opening you may want to indicate to the employer that you would be willing to start in another position. Let him know you are willing to learn rather than having an "I can do this and nothing else" attitude.

If you fail to get a job after trying a few times, don't give up. Be persistent. Working hard at finding a job will make you feel part of the "working world" rather than part of the unemployed.

One high school vocational teacher, who had worked in personnel positions and as a professional business woman for 18 years before she became a teacher, told me:

> I know what employers look for when high school girls apply for jobs. *The first thing is appearance, always.* Is she clean, neat, and dressed appropriately? No dangling earrings. The second point is her voice. It should be clear, audible, and well-modulated. Girls should never change to a mousey, low-tone, bashful-sounding voice. Speak up! Next, the employer will evaluate the girl according to the application form. If blanks are left,

lines drawn through writing, and answers scribbled, she will be judged by this. Last, he will check her qualifications.

# EMPLOYERS TELL ALL!!!

Employers who have high school girls working for them have some interesting things to say. Do you dare keep on reading? I called a nursing home first. The dietary supervisor said she's had very good results with her high school help. "Good success with them!" Then she continued, "But the floor supervisor may not tell you the same." She was right. The other woman wasn't as impressed as the first one.

"We do check references," she stated. "If they have been dependable, more than likely we will hire them. Reference is important." She went on to say, "The main thing is to do a good job and when you leave, give a notice." Girls leaving without telling her was her pet peeve. "We are dealing with people not machinery. They must be cared for," was her reasoning. When I asked what other problems came up, I had a feeling she would tell me.

"Personal conflicts," she continued. "If the girls have trouble at school they will, at times, bring it to work with them—a lack of maturity. And if a girl stands back with arms crossed and won't ask questions, she won't stay long," she concluded.

"Have you ever had to terminate a girl?" I asked.

"Never," she said, "but I do call the teacher and ask for a conference for some of the girls. We work very closely with the school. Say, if they will not take directions, their discipline then is a conference with the teacher."

The manager of one large department store that

hires high school girls gave some of their rules and regulations. He said, "The majority of the girls are very good." But he offered this advice in the same breath, "We want them to present themselves in an aggressive way to customers and remember the customer comes first, even before friends that 'pop' in."

Excessive talking was the first offense he mentioned. A corrective interview is their first step after a breach of ethics. Then, if a girl keeps breaking the rules a "weeding out" begins. If you worked in this store, you could put yourself out of a job by the following violations:

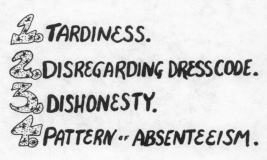

**1. TARDINESS.**

**2. DISREGARDING DRESS CODE.**

**3. DISHONESTY.**

**4. PATTERN of ABSENTEEISM.**

Another employer came down a little harder on teenage help. She, the owner of the establishment, began by saying: "Kids have not been taught to have responsibility. My biggest complaint is their lack of pride in their work. I also oppose one being too timid or one being indignant. One has the attitude, 'You owe me a job, how much do you pay?' the other, too shy to lift her head, can't work for looking down at the floor."

"Not thorough and won't follow directions," she responded when I asked what else bugged her about the young hired help. "Ten minutes after I give directions I can walk back through and it is already forgotten and ignored. It's very frustrating," she spoke sadly. "I'd like to be more than just the boss to them, but they won't let me."

God is not only interested in your finding the right job, He is also concerned about how "Christian" you are in your daily tasks. You should seek His guidance in this as definitely as you do in job hunting and choosing a job. Your work record will follow you all your life. If you keep a good, clean record you will have a good resume any time you need it.

Most theorists agree that, more than anything else, successful work experience helps a young person resolve the conflicts of dependency and establish an independent identity. Once your competence is proven and confirmed it is a rewarding role for you. The identity you thought you would never find begins to show through to you and to the world. You don't have to holler, "Hey! It's me!" anymore.

The breakaway years of adolescence, when you are growing *toward* independence and *away* from your familiar sheltered homelife, may cause you to feel off balance. Speaking of the teenage girl, the director of counseling for the American Institute of Family Relations in Los Angeles said, "She has one foot at home and one foot out the door. It's hard to keep your balance this way."

God cares about this period in your life. He desires to give you perfect balance as you follow His instructions in His personal message to you, in the Bible. Anytime you begin to totter you may dial Him direct (*toil*-free) and talk to Him "person to person."

Read James 1:5 to be assured God has a bountiful supply of wisdom for you if you ask Him. All the work experience you get will help you choose a career, if you want to be a career girl.

## Chapter Ten

When I was a little girl there was a certain game we enjoyed playing better than any others. It was a game of make-believe called "play-like."

One of us would say, "Play like we're at the store and this little woman comes in and she falls and breaks her leg and I'm a nurse and. . . ." In our fantasy world we would go into action. The grocery shelves had to be stocked, the bandages gathered, and someone had to get dressed to look like a grandmother. For hours we would play one role after another.

The next time I would be a secretary, then a schoolteacher, and later maybe a hairdresser.

I did say when I was a *little* girl we played these games. When I was a teenager we didn't "play-like" any more, but daydreaming took its place. It was a grown-up name for "play-like."

In the city where I grew up it was the "in" thing to enroll for Hawaiian steel guitar lessons. To pay for my lessons I worked in the music studio on Saturdays as the receptionist. There were several classrooms close to my desk and I could watch and sometimes hear the instructors. One was a young lady I dearly adored. At that time I dreamed of a music career. Over and over in my mind I built my own music studio in the shape of a guitar! I visualized a giant guitar turned on its side with classrooms spaced all along the neck. Each fret on the neck of the guitar would be a separate room with a solid, lovely glass front. Only the bars of the frets would separate the glass partitions.

I *knew* what my career was going to be—a music teacher, forever and always. I went as far as finishing the 68 guitar lessons of the first course and starting on the professional course when I was 13 years old. Then we moved to another state where most of the people had never seen a girl play a guitar. The puzzled looks on some of our friends' faces when my dad insisted I play for them, caused my ambition for a music career to fade rapidly.

In a way, some girls play the game of make-believe all their lives because they never decide to settle on any particular field of interest. They never train or learn skills. They only "play-like" whatever suits their fancy and is popular at the time. This could happen to you if you blindly ignore all the career opportunities, refuse to research, and fail to develop any one interest.

You may be thinking, "But I don't want a career. I want a home and a family. I'm not the career girl type." You may plan to work only long enough to buy new clothes and make preparations for the prettiest wedding in the world—yours!

Raising and nurturing children is a fine goal and a challenge but it certainly takes parenting skills too. On the other hand, you may need this information more than you think because there is a great possibility you will have to work sometime in your life. To be totally unprepared would be a very difficult adjustment.

Chances are 8 out of 10 you will work a while before marriage and return to work after your last child enters school, for a total of possibly 30 years. Are you surprised? These predictions came from a government booklet. Many times the wife changes her mind about a career, for one reason or another. Sometimes it is to help her husband further his education or advance his training. Or a wife is unexpectedly left a widow and has to work. It is wiser and much easier to develop a skill while you are young.

# Christian Careers

A career can be an occupation or a profession but does not necessarily have to be either one. A profession involves a liberal, scientific, or artistic education. An occupation means little more than one's regular or immediate job. A career is often a learned skill or simply an ability developed fully.

God loves to have your abilities to work with. After

all they were a gift from Him. As you begin to pray for God's guidance and perfect will in this important time of your life, Christian careers should be considered first.

I have a young friend who is in her early twenties—an assistant pastor's wife and a nurse. I asked her opinion about careers for young women and her answer started me thinking a different way.

She said: "Living for Jesus is the most exciting career any Christian can profess and it must be the first one followed. Other careers will fall in place, if you put the desires of your heart within the Lord's hands and then love Him and serve Him. Your desires will be fulfilled joyfully and miraculously." She went on to say, "Your choice of a career is also His choice for you. He wants your happiness. He wants you fulfilled."

It happened that way for her! In high school she worked in a day-care center. She had a desire to be a nurse. The week she gave her notice to quit her job the Lord led her into the beginning of her career. She received a call from a local doctor's office and was asked if she would be interested in "on-the-job" training as a medical assistant. She was recommended by a teacher because she had proven herself.

What are some careers for girls in the Christian field? Do you think of missionary work or a pulpit ministry? There are many dedicated women doing both, but there are other directions in Christian careers. Professional Christian singers and musicians are in great demand right now. Women can fill the position of minister of music and some make a career of it.

How about church child-care directors or teachers, salespersons for Christian merchandise, or a career in Christian art? Young women can effectively be public relations (PR) people for Christian associations. In the Christian writing field there are multiple doors open.

All of these Christian careers have related branches you could get into. They too require spe-

cialized training and developing—and that's left up
to you.

A young girl in Albuquerque whom I admire very
much set her goal to be a journalist while she was in
high school. I was pleased that she stuck with her
choice and kept taking courses that would help her.
Recently I was told she was reporting a church-
related story for an assignment in college. She edited
the film and wrote the script.

But someone said, "Dream with your feet on the
ground." Your dream will never come true unless
you make it happen. On the way to successfully
fulfilling a dream there are many necessary inter-
mediate steps. One young woman I know dreams of
having a music career and she is working in an office
to finance the developing of her chosen career. Right

now, in little ways, you can work toward your future. Go to the library and research your "dream." Take the steps to make it come true.

I hear girls complain about the boring classes of science, math, and other subjects at school. They wail, "Why do I need to take this or that?" If you decide not to develop these abilities any further, you automatically cut your options by 60 percent, says one authority. There are more careers waiting for those with expertise and training in science and math. Boring classes give you a chance to acquire lots of knowledge plus discipline and maturity to achieve your ultimate goal.

You do want options? Don't be afraid to pursue any career that interests you. So you want to be a commercial airline pilot. Don't laugh. Young women are breaking through every day. It was exciting for me to watch two young women pilots being interviewed on TV after their first overseas flight. One way to stay in your make-believe world is to feel you can never do what you really want to do. Circumstances, society's needs, and your own dreams are all subject to change. It simply makes sense to keep your options open.

# Other Choices

It is estimated that 80 percent of the nation's jobs do not require a college degree. For every doctor, for example, there are many more other related health personnel urgently needed.

The health field shows strong growth—especially for optometrists, dental assistants and hygienists, and nurses. Careers for health administrators, emergency medical technicians, and medical record clerks also look promising. Once trained you'll be entering the steadily growing health sciences field.

A forecast says competition will remain keen in entertainment, journalism, photography, and aviation. This means you will have to work a little harder if you choose one of those careers. In office careers, receptionists, secretaries, computer programmers, systems analysts, and banking positions look promising.

The secretarial job was once the only stepping-stone to executive posts. It still serves that purpose. Some young women, known as "progressional secretaries," actually go into secretarial jobs with the understanding that they are being apprenticed for other types of work. One California savings and loan association has chosen half its department heads and branch managers from women who began working as secretaries. The Bank of America encourages its secretaries to enroll in a career-counseling program to earn promotions.

The most ambitious secretaries these days seek a formal rating of CPS (Certified Professional Secretary), which can be achieved by passing a 2-day, six-part exam dealing with topics ranging from behavioral science in business to accounting.

For the first time in history young women have a full array of choices. You can be the best you can be and you don't have to choose between marriage and a career. You can have both if you so desire.

I read about a lady physician in Sydney, Australia who has some beautiful thoughts on the attitude of Jesus about women's traditional roles. Lynette Wark sees a connection between her commitment to Christ and the rest of her life. She says Jesus treated women as He treated all people—with equality. A woman witnessed that He was the Messiah even though Judaic law did not allow women to bear legal witness. A woman was the first to witness His resurrection. Jesus didn't see women as just childbearers and housekeepers. When a woman blessed His mother for giving birth, He replied: "Yea, rather, blessed are they that hear the word of God, and keep it" (Luke 11:28). When Martha wanted Jesus to tell Mary to help with the cooking instead of just listening to Him speak, Jesus replied: "There is really only one thing worth being concerned about. Mary has discovered it" (Luke 10:42, *The Living Bible*).

The best assurance that your dreams will come true is to live daily within God's will. Don't you think you should take time to carefully choose a career in which you can reach out and help others in some measure? This will bring you real gratification.

To *gratify* is to please and to give liberally, whereas satisfaction suggests giving just enough and no more—a state of mind that is merely content. A job can be satisfying but a Christian's career should bring gratification.

The career you choose, carefully and prayerfully, should bring you more than satisfaction. It should be:

✔ **1.** STIMULATING & EXCITING.

**2.** GROWTH PROMOTING.

**3.** CREATIVE & PRODUCTIVE.

**4.** GRATIFYING...

MEMORIZE: PROVERBS 3:6

# Chapter Eleven

# PICK-UP STICKS

Your whole life at this point may seem to be made of nothing but decisions. The college scene is not without questions and choices either. You've hardly decided what high school subjects to take when you are asked about college. Your course of action determines all your happy or unhappy tomorrows.

You may be wondering: "Should I go to college? where? for how long? How can I finance it? Can I get admitted? How hard are the entrance exams? If I get in, can I make it? What is God's plan for me?"

The answers to these questions, and many others, you hold in your hand like a bundle of pickup sticks. Once the sticks are dropped and they fall as they will, the game begins.

Pickup Sticks is a game enjoyed by all ages. It is a low-pressure, simple game played with 31 slim, different colored sticks. Each color is worth a certain number of points. The player holds all the sticks in one hand and lets them fall. They have to remain in the position they fall—stacked and lying crooked in a jumbled heap. The object of the game is to pick up as many as possible, one at a time, without disturbing the others.

The sticks have been dropped. Colleges are built. Rules are set. Entrance tests are approved. The cost is determined. You can change none of those; they are out of your control. Nor can you determine how

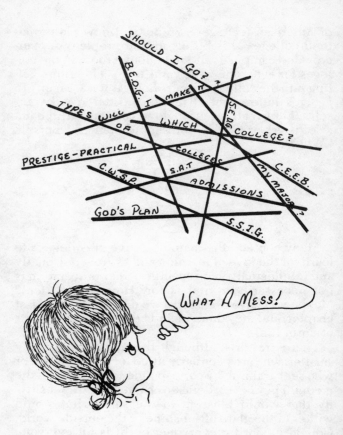

the sticks will fall. They fall differently for every person. All you can do is carefully pick up the sticks one by one, enjoy the game, and wait and see if you win.

The world today is a very interesting place. It is a wonderful time to be living. When Harvard College opened its doors in 1636, education was reserved for those few destined to become ministers, doctors, or lawyers. In the early part of the 19th century, less than 5 percent of the college-age population attended college. According to a recent Gallup survey of American teenagers, 75 percent now plan to attend college. This brings up the problem of over-crowded campuses and not enough room in the colleges for everyone who wants to go. Therefore, getting into the college of your choice is not a "snap." In fact, it's quite a fight, all things considered. Ask yourself, "Do I really want to go to college?" If the answer is yes or maybe, you should then ask yourself, "Why?"

Many contend the main objective of college is to learn for the love of learning and to grow personally and intellectually, and specific career preparation is not necessarily a vital factor. How do you feel? Maybe you have dreams, as we discussed in the last chapter, and they don't include those hallowed halls of dorm life.

There are girls, although the number is getting smaller, who are peculiarly fitted for staying home or who seek training by correspondence or through the media. They have a delicate character and a sensitivity that would blossom in the shade, but would wither in the glare of sunshine or the outside world. College is not for everyone, but it is for everyone who sincerely wants it. Ask yourself:

 Do I really want to go to college, or am I planning on it to please someone else?

 Is my reason for going to college just to get away from home?

 Am I going to college for lack of anything else to do?

If you have a better reason for going to college, such as, "To learn something to help me have a life of service to God and people as I train for a livelihood," you should start checking it all out early—long before you finish high school.

I've often heard a minister say, "God doesn't do anything for you that you can do for yourself." From the beginning of this book you have been advised and encouraged to ask God for His will in your choices. But you have noticed He doesn't dump His will on you. You are the key—and the only key—that will unlock His plan or His will for you.

College choices are to be faced. God will not check all the details for you. He is not going to pile on your lap "College Times" (facts for your future from the college board), "On Your Own" (a guide to getting started after high school), or "Senior Crossroads" and the "Student Bulletin" (prepared and produced by Educational Testing Service [ETS]).

God *is* interested in whether or not you can afford college, but He won't read aloud to you all the financial aid programs. (Basic Educational Opportunity Grant [BEOG] and College Work-study Program [CWSP] are two of the ones available.) Neither will He fill out your application for a grant or go to the admissions office and say for you, "She's eligible for a scholarship or a loan!"

God cares if you pass your entrance examinations, but He is not going to write the answers in your Scholastic Aptitude Test (SAT). Getting into college depends on you.

# CHOOSE A COLLEGE

Before you decide on the college you want to attend, you should know there are many different types of colleges and universities. There are thousands of state colleges, district or city colleges, independent institutions, and denominational institutions. A few years ago it was estimated the number was growing at a rate of 50 a year.

We have 2-year colleges, 4-year colleges, and 5-, 6-, 7-, and 8-year colleges. I have a friend who went to college for 8 years. She became the first woman military chaplain (Air Force) in her denomination. Public institutions are growing far more rapidly than private colleges. They have a much lower tuition rate and at the same time provide the student with a greater variety of courses. But if you are willing or able to pay the additional costs, you may get the type of education more suited to your needs in a private institution.

American higher education from its very inception has been church related. Of the hundreds of denomination-controlled colleges, many are nonsectarian in the sense that students of all denominations are admitted. Denominational institutions are a powerful factor in American education.

CAMPUS SURVIVAL KIT

A Christian young person can be an important influence on any college campus. This week one of my neighbors, a sophomore at Stephen F. Austin State University, came home for spring break. She had transferred from a denominational college and I was anxious to hear about her adjustment.

I knew when I looked into her sparkling blue eyes what she was going to tell me would be good. This tiny-featured, perfect-figured teenager had not changed much in looks since I had first met her 6 years ago. She was even more poised and lovely. Everything she said revealed a noticeable spiritual growth.

"My being a Christian," she began in her soft voice, "I didn't know how I would be accepted. I kept thinking, how in the world can I relate to these girls? But you know, the Lord opened up a way through music. One girl played the guitar and we went to the lounge and I played the piano and she played the guitar. We got acquainted through that. Every chance I get I just begin sharing," she continued. "The Lord has taught me so much. He showed me to go to the spiritually hungry first before I tried to witness to those who were uninterested."

"Oh, let me tell you about my Bible study," she said excitedly. She explained how she had started her own Bible study and the Lord had blessed her and others were being helped.

She wanted to share one incident in particular with me. A girl from another state had come to visit for a week and stayed with a friend in the dorm. When my neighbor met her she quickly detected a spiritual hunger and a need in her life. She invited the guest to her Bible study and the girl said she would call and let her know.

She thought it was a rebuff but she hurried in after her last class to wait for the call. When it was time to leave for the Bible study, she still had not heard from her. With a heavy heart she left, telling her roommate, "If my new friend calls, tell her I'm on my way and I'll pick her up in front of the dorm." Not really expecting her to be there, she drove in that direction, saying a prayer and wondering how she could ever reach her again. But she was there! Standing on the corner in the rain, with her Bible under her arm!

"I didn't really want to go. I didn't know what I was doing out there—with my Bible in my hand," she later said.

Campus ministries are the Christian's survival kit in secular colleges. My neighbor belongs to Chi Alpha, a college ministry, and a prayer group, besides her own Bible study. I asked her about other campus ministries and was happily surprised when she could think of 12 different ones. Several were interdenominational, which made me especially glad. How thrilling to see the day when Spirit-filled Christians are ready to say, "If you are a Christian, you are my sister or my brother."

One minister on a religious show said for every young person embracing a foreign religion five are turning to Christianity. The number should be greater, and it will be as Christian young people continue to be led by the Holy Spirit, as my neighbor was.

The same girl told me, "I do a lot of listening . . . and listening, while they pour out their problems." She told me one girl had been smoking marijuana and hiding it from her roommate. She put a towel at the bottom of the door and locked the door while she was smoking. Her guilt bothered her and one day my friend just asked her, "Are you smoking marijuana?" When she confessed it and wanted to talk, my friend shared Jesus with her. She won her confidence by being concerned about her and letting her talk as long as she needed to. This can be a real ministry.

"When I went to the new school I never said anything about drinking or smoking, but they know I don't do it and they never ask me," my friend re-

# Is there life After High School?

"Trust in the Lord with all thine heart; and lean not unto thine own understanding" (Proverbs 3:5).

marked. "They even try to shield me from seeing what goes on and tease me a little about being my guardian angel. We can't decide who is whose—if they are mine, or I am theirs," she chuckled.

It's difficult, in the final analysis, to calculate the true value of a college education. The value—or lack of it—depends on the individual, and that is you. If you play the game fairly and move each pickup stick as you come to it, you should get to the one that counts the most, "God's plan for me." Then you're the winner!

# Chapter Twelve

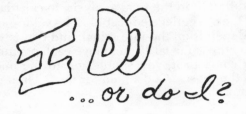

Wilt thou have this man to be your lawful and wedded husband? Do you promise to love and cherish him, in sickness and in health, for richer for poorer, for better for worse, and forsaking all others, keep thee only unto him, so long as you both shall live?

I do? As long as we both shall live? As long as we both shall *love,* maybe—but for life? in sickness? how sick? To love and cherish. . . .

To cherish? I'm not especially fond of him now when he disagrees with me. When he wants to go to the game at his school and not mine. When he wants a cheeseburger and I want Chinese food.

To love, as long as he stays home with me and doesn't go off someplace working on his old car.

To wait until the marriage vows are said before you start thinking all this through would be a little late. When you get to the altar, the last thing you need in that pretty veiled head of yours is a brawl going on, with doubt knocking Cupid around.

Love and romance are in every girl's dreams. She plans for and talks about her own wedding long before the possibility of marriage. There's nothing really wrong with this, except reality is often hidden in the reverie. Facts are overlooked completely and dreams are shattered early in a young life when

*To Marry...*

*or*

*To Wait.*

teenagers jump into marriage unprepared and with high expectations. When the honeymoon is over and two people begin to share the same house and everything in the house, plus having to share everything that goes on in their lives, puff goes the dream! Ann Landers says: "All marriages are happy, it's living together that's tough."

When you prepare for it and build up to a maturity in an assortment of areas, marriage can be more than your most fanciful dreams. But it takes time, and it takes energy directed toward the project.

Love, romance, marriage, and teenagers—what a combination! I'm not against marriage. Mine has been successful. I don't resist love. It still keeps my world and yours revolving. I don't oppose young people in any way. Some of my closest friends are teenagers. But I have observed many shaky teenage marriages. For that reason and several others, I advise against it.

There are certain essential elements that make up the best marriage structure. I want very much for you to see how you can lay your own foundation, a layer at a time, so your marriage (if that is in the will of God for you) will not be a trembling, quivering union, falling apart all too soon. The more years you spend working on it, the firmer the foundation.

Christ the Rock, should be the bottom layer everything else is built on. A oneness in Christ is the principal base on which any relationship should be built. To know, when the time does come, that the person you intend to spend the rest of your life with has experienced the new birth and puts Christ first, should be your number one concern.

Then there's love. What is love? The answers are varied, ranging from infatuation and crushes to sex and submission. I feel sure you already know there are different kinds of love. If you don't, the first time your "one and only" touches your shoulder lightly and your heart beats faster than you can count its throbs, you will know. You will discover it is not the same as your father's loving pat on the shoulder.

Mac and Vivian Rice wrote a delightful book for Christian young people, *When Can I Say, "I Love You"?* (Chicago: Moody Press, 1977). They explain that the Greeks had several words for love while, unfortunately, we try to make do with only one. Three important types of love are represented by the Greek words *agape, phileo,* and *eros.*

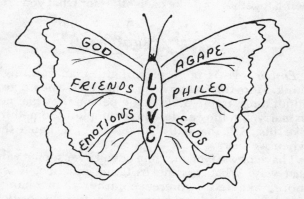

Which of these three kinds of love is necessary for a happy marriage? All three of them are. "It is like a three-legged stool. If any leg breaks, the stool collapses," the authors concluded.

*Agape* is normally used for God's love for man,

man's love for God, and man's Christian love for his fellowman.

*Phileo* indicates that you enjoy the company of the other person, such as in a friendship. Both *agape* and *phileo* love are in the Bible.

*Eros*, the other principal Greek word for love, refers to physical, sexual love, usually set going by the emotions. This is the only meaning some young people attach to love. Although the word is not in the Bible, it does not mean God is silent on the subject of sexual love. He invented it you know. He also made the rules.

*Agape* love is part of the fruit of the Spirit, the harvest produced in God's children. You should have this love for all people and to a much greater degree for the one you marry.

Certainly there must be *phileo* love in a marriage. This kind of love says, "I want to be with you. Let's sit by the fireplace and eat pizza," or, "It's nice to have you with me as we drive along." You must enjoy being together and like each other for what you are.

Testing Ground

*Phileo* love is more meaningful than you might think. More times than I can count I have heard girls admit undesirable traits in the person they planned to marry, but they ended their complaint something like this, "Oh, that will change," or, "I'll change that when we marry."

I have news: Not one time have I ever seen it work that way. Whatever the irritating practice, it will more than likely increase rather than change. Whether it is a critical tongue, a pouting disposition, or annoying eating habits, you better decide if you can live with it, because you will have to. Your magic wand goes out the door with the swept-up rice from the wedding. You had better *like* the person you marry a lot.

*Eros* is the blind love you hear people talk about that you think will never strike you. The minute rockets and bells go off, blindness sets in. That's why I talked about *agape* and *phileo* love first. A marriage foundation needs all three kinds of love. If you choose a companion for life with your eyes closed, by *eros* love only, in most cases, your eyes will be rudely opened soon after marriage.

Such a beautiful mystical relationship marriage is! Your virginity is a gift that can be given only one time and to one person. Save this precious gift, tied with your heartstrings, for the special young man you will share your life with.

The English novelist, Barbara Cartland, just celebrated the sale of 100 million books! Her writings are mostly romantic love stories. Her ideals were challenged recently. "No one goes to bed in your books," was the charge.

"Yes they do," she replied curtly, "with a ring on their finger!"

Another testing ground for a happy marriage is found in your own home. How do you get along with

the other members in your family? Do you ever resent having them under your feet when you want to be alone? Could you do without the mess your sister constantly leaves? Can you say kindly, "Please move your clothes off my bed," or do you throw them in a heap in the corner? Where is it the hardest for you to live a Christian life? At home? Until you can act like an adult in family relationships, you are nowhere near ready for marriage. Your husband is going to become as commonplace as members of your family.

There is no use looking for complete emotional maturity, but are you ready for *his* brand of immaturity? rages? sulking? jealousy? self-centeredness? Does he goof off instead of working? Is he no more ready for marriage than you?

Those who fare best in their marriage (1) yield to one another; (2) have a balance of togetherness and separation, releasing each other to be his own unique person; and (3) have no power struggle, sharing the decisionmaking.

##
To Be Chosen

In the love story of Isaac and Rebekah there are several similarities to what has been said about laying a good foundation for marriage. Read Genesis 24 to enjoy the details of this storybook marriage.

A young suitor seeks a wife. The search begins. Prayer and asking God's guidance are the first step. A concern for God's perfect will is evident.

A girl enters the scene—a very fair to look upon young virgin. She makes a definite impression by her kindness, in word and deed. Her hospitality is offered sincerely and politely. Gifts are accepted graciously and with gratitude.

In her home, family ties are proper. A good sister-brother relationship exists. Normal reaction from her mother indicates love in the family. The mother pleads, "Let the damsel abide with us a few days, at the least ten" (v. 55). The independent young woman exhibits maturity when she is asked, "Wilt thou go?" and she answers, "I will go" (v. 58).

The last verse of the chapter says: "And Isaac . . . took Rebekah, and she became his wife; and he loved her: and Isaac was comforted" (v. 67).

Now is that a love story? Rebekah was ready and prepared to be chosen. I like verse 50 which says: "The thing proceedeth from the Lord."

## How Old's Too Young?

The anthem of your generation may be, "Marriage, a Way Out," but until the foundation has been laid for a permanent, lifelong relationship you would do well to sing another song. There are no shortcuts to maturity. When you're young you go through different stages. Marriage doesn't change that. You are maturing when you visualize the results of your actions before you perform them.

I hope you don't throw the book down when I tell you God's approval and timing should be at the very top in "The Fine Art of Choosing a Mate." I grew up in a church full of girls about my age and only one or two eligible young men. My mother called in prayer the names of several Christian young men who lived in neighboring towns. She said, "Lord, I believe you are able to send one of these good Christian boys for my daughter to go with." Soon we changed pastors and it happened that the new pastor's son was one of the names she had called in prayer. After we were married she told me.

When decision time rolls around and you have to decide whether to marry or to wait, and that special guy tries to convince you a diamond is a girl's best friend, you will know the facts.

How old is too young? When you can say, "The thing proceedeth from the Lord," you're old enough. In the meantime, work on becoming marriageable. If you are chosen for marital bliss or if God has a special purpose for you to remain single, the foundation is good for any life.

GOD'S TIMING & APPROVAL

TESTING GROUND          FAMILY RELATIONS

THREE KINDS OF LOVE

LORDSHIP OF CHRIST

Chapter Thirteen

"You don't really think God speaks to people today, do you?"

The question surprised me, coming from a Christian friend sitting in my den. I had not discussed it with anyone but I thought all Christians heard from God once in a while.

"Why, yes, I believe God speaks to His children," I answered quickly. I began debating how to share my "sacred" experiences with a skeptical heart without sounding superspiritual.

"But in an audible voice?" my friend's unbelieving tone bounced back at me.

"Well, not often. But yes, I've heard His audible voice," I said. As she raised her eyebrows my mind raced back to the thundering, booming voice that had seemed to push the walls of my bedroom out—the first time I heard His audible voice.

Before I could relate my story, the woman's husband came and they left. I kept thinking about the times I had heard the Lord speak to me. Sometimes it was through a dynamic revelation. A few times He showed me visions and gave me answers from the Scriptures. Other times it was in a still small voice. And many times there was just a deep assurance in my inner being, a feeling, an impression that let me know it had to be God speaking.

Teenage Christians everywhere should listen for a message from heaven too. You may never hear an audible voice, but if God wants to talk to you in any of His wonderful ways, you can't hear unless you are listening.

*Dake's Annotated Reference Bible* (Lawrenceville, GA: Dake Bible Sales, Inc.) notes the *voice* of the Lord is referred to 142 times. This doesn't include the hundreds of "thus saith the Lords" and other expressions of His speaking.

Adam, Abraham, Moses, Elijah, Isaiah, Ezekiel, Daniel, Peter, James, John, and Paul all heard the actual voice of the Lord, the Scriptures point out.

I am not saying these experiences are for everyone. If God chooses to speak in an extraordinary manner, it is blessed, but He is more apt to speak to you through His Word, your minister, your conscience, or in a number of other ways. It makes you no greater or lesser in God's sight however He speaks to you. It matters only that you obey Him.

Some young people think God doesn't speak except to "call" a person to be a missionary or preacher. He does speak to people to do a special work, but He also calls each of us to discipleship and a life of separation. To the willing and obedient heart He makes it clear that separation without service is empty.

Our youth pastor said this week: "God is choosing people who are saying unreservedly, 'I'll go,' or, 'I'll do. . . .' God is looking for those who will say, 'Yes, Lord,' for whatever He asks. He is not looking for a new spiritual master race. . . . In submitting, you will go at God's pace and in God's direction to be anything that He wants you to be. . . . You can't live in the natural totally and expect to be used in the supernatural."

God desires to use the talents you have and He may talk to you about this. The artist who did the illustrations for this book prayed before the job and told God, "I don't have much to offer, but what I have I want to give to You, Lord. Take my artistic ability if You can use it."

Later she told me she couldn't believe she had been bold enough to say to me, "I feel like the Lord

"...MY SHEEP HEAR MY VOICE..."

wants me to tell you I am an artist," when we had just met each other. God spoke to her after she said, "Take what I have and use it, Lord." It's two-way communication.

Several times the Scriptures clearly state that God heard men. A child crying was the first voice on record to be heard by God. It was Ishmael in Genesis 21:17. Manoah, Samson's father, "entreated the Lord, and said, O my Lord, let the man of God which thou didst send come again unto us, and teach us what we shall do unto the child that shall be born. And *God hearkened to the voice* of Manoah" (Judges 13:8, 9).

Jonah said about his joyride in the stomach of the big fish, "I cried by reason of mine affliction unto the Lord, and he heard me; out of the belly of hell cried I, and *thou heardest my voice*" (Jonah 2:2).

The incident that stands out to me was when God listened to Joshua and "the sun stood still, and the moon stayed. . . . And there was no day like that before it or after it, that *the Lord hearkened unto the voice of a man:* for the Lord fought for Israel" (Joshua 10:13, 14).

Not long ago I was conducting ladies' leadership

training when one of the speakers, for no apparent reason, said, "We must stop and pray for the country of Senegal." As I prayed from the front pew God gave me a vision.

I saw the outline of this country very plainly as I visualized the continent of Africa. Hot winds were blowing across the land, scorching and bending the ready-to-harvest grain to the ground. As we prayed I knew in my spirit it was the power of the enemy. Suddenly a very thin silver wall was raised at the border of that country, blocking the destructive winds of oppression. God was showing us that in response to our prayers He would raise a protective shield.

## MY SHEEP KNOW MY VOICE

One of the times God spoke gently, yet forcefully, to me was through His Word. I had an invitation to go to Panama as a counselor with a youth group. I wanted to go but I had a husband, a 12-year-old daughter, and a grown son at home. I was torn between my obligations to my family and going with a Christian group of kids to witness.

One Sunday night I was sitting alone quietly praying when the thought came strongly to my mind and wouldn't leave, "My sheep know My voice, and they will follow Me." Before I realized what I was saying I gasped, "All the way to Panama, Lord?" But I didn't receive an answer. My mind wasn't settled. At the close of the service we knelt at the front of the church in worship and a lady who was new in our church tapped me on the shoulder and said, "I don't know what this means but I feel that the Lord wants me to tell you, 'My sheep know My voice and they will follow Me.'"

*The Living Bible* says: "He walks ahead of them;

and they follow him, for they recognize his voice" (John 10:4).

I was troubled, so when I got home I went straight to our bedroom and pulled a promise from the Scripture box. I half expected it to read, "My sheep know My voice . . . ," but it didn't say that. It was a definite answer though because of the way it pierced me when I read, "And the Lord said . . . , Go on . . ." (Exodus 17:5). The word *go* was capitalized and stood out. I got my Bible and read the surrounding verses. I saw it had been spoken to Moses during a distressing time of his life. As I read the preceding verse, "Moses cried unto the Lord, saying, What shall I do. . . ?" it burned in my heart as much as if my name had been inserted in it. I went to Panama in the perfect will of God.

A few years later when I had the opportunity to go to Tanzania, East Africa on the same kind of trip, the Lord verified His will about it twice with the same Scripture passage, "My sheep . . ."—once before I left home and once on the way, between New York and London. We were over the ocean when I pulled out some literature that had been given to us at orientation in Newark, New Jersey. The first page was a poem, written by an elderly Christian writer, especially for the teams going to 15 countries that summer. In tiny print across the top was: "My sheep hear my voice, and I know them, and they follow me" (John 10:27).

I don't have to tell you I was closer to heaven than the shiny new British Caledonian plane I was gliding along in, about 35,000 feet in the air. My tears kept me from reading for a while.

God didn't speak all these times, one right after the other. What I've shared with you happened over a period of 20 years.

There were also other times God spoke to me. Once, while conducting a revival in California, we were staying in an upstairs garage apartment. In the stillness of the night, after everyone else was asleep, I was praying. Hot tears soaked my pillow. All of a sudden I heard a "booming, thunderous" voice say, "Ye are the light of the world!" The walls seemed to vibrate and I knew our two children and my husband must have heard it and been awakened. But all was still.

Then a brown flat map unfurled across the wall. I watched as mountains arose with sharp peaks and dangerous drop-offs. The crevices of the earth and the valleys were pallid and treacherous. I visualized people trying to step across the crevices and ravines and climb the tall mountains with no light to show them the way. Many of them were about to fall; they were slipping and groping because of the darkness.

As suddenly as it had appeared, the map disappeared. In its place was a gigantic revolving world globe in full color, lit up like a neon light. I could hear, "Ye are the light of the world," echoing in my heart. I questioned momentarily, "Lord, I thought You were the Light of the world." But instantly the sweetest bidding came to me. I began to realize all believers are the light of Christ; lighting up their part of the world, showing people where to walk and how to walk without slipping and falling.

"Ye are the light of the world."

In the Scriptures you will find, "Ye are the light of the world" (Matthew 5:14). In John 8:12 Jesus said, "I am the light of the world." We are the light because He is the Light. If you are a light you are going to show someone the way.

Winkie Pratney, in *A Handbook for Followers of Jesus* (Minneapolis: Bethany Fellowship, Inc., 1977), says the Bible is the story of common men and women who found the will of God. Jacob met the angel of the Lord. Joseph had dreams. Moses saw a burning bush and Paul saw a blinding light. Little Samuel heard a voice and John saw a vision.

# Check List

-Yes-No-Maybe-

❀ Have I talked to God
   lately? . . . . . . . . . . ☑ ☐ ☐

❀ Has He ever spoken
   to me? . . . . . . . . . . ☑ ☐ ☐

❀ Is communication
   clogged between us? ☐ ☐ ☐
                    sometimes

❀ I hear His voice
   in the Bible,
   directly to me . . . . ☐ ☐ ☐
                    don't know

❀ I know God will
   speak to me in all
   my choices if I
   allow Him to . . . . . . ☑ ☐ ☐

You may never experience any of these but you will hear the Lord speak to you if you talk to Him and have an obedient heart. He talks when you talk to Him, and sometimes when you don't. From your mouth to God's ears, a, "Here am I, Lord, for whatever You wish," will bring you adventuresome living and lead you down many exciting paths.

As you learn to recognize His voice you can expect direction and guidance in every choice you have to make. Each decision can be an open door to discipleship.